Les Petites Dames de Mode

An Adventure in Design

Les Petites Dames de Mode

An Adventure in Design

JOHN R. BURBIDGE

foreword by Elizabeth Ann Coleman

Reverie

PUBLISHING COMPANY

To Cile

the "Grande Dame" in my life for fifty-two wonderful years

and

our five children—Christine, Susan, Richard, Anne and Jenifer,

our three sons-in-law—Kevin, Al and Gary,

and our seven grandchildren—

Sean, Ryan, Brenna, Stephanie, Peter, Claire and Colin,

all who have lit up those fifty-two years.

First Edition/First Printing

To purchase additional copies of this book, please contact:
Reverie Publishing Company
130 Wineow Street
Cumberland, MD 21502
888-721-4999

Library of Congress Control Number 2003093611
ISBN 1-932485-06-6

Photos page 2, 140, 141: Courtesy of Fairfield Historical Society
Packing photos page 141: Robert Young
All other photos: John R. Burbidge

Project Editor: Krystyna Poray Goddu

Design: Anna Christian

Printed and bound in Korea

Contents

In Appreciation

Although this is the story of one person's adventure in design, I have not been alone in the journey, and am most grateful to those who have given me their encouragment and help. This book had been lurking around in my mind for some time and I had suffered the rebuffs of several publishers, as have so many others. It was through Joyce Miko of the American Academy of Doll Artists, a long-time admirer of Les Dames, that I met Krystyna Poray Goddu of Reverie Publishing, who unhesitantly offered to be my publisher, and the "show" was finally on the road.

I am grateful to my daughters Christine and Jenifer who, being computer-wise, have always been available to put my words, which I type out on my venerable Olympia typewriter, on to high-tech discs.

Not as yet having entered the computer world, I am equally indebted to my next-door granddaughter Brenna who, at the ripe old age of thirteen, operates my website and email with all the expertise of youth.

High on my "thank-you" list is my son Richard, who has created many of my exhibit props with great skill and inventiveness.

I am also indebted to my son-in-law Kevin, who has from time to time turned his talented hands to resolving certain mechanical problems beyond my thread-and-needle abilities.

I would like to express my appreciation to both Loretta Tenaglia and Lewis Anthony DeLuca, who have been my wife's hairdressers over the years, and have also worked their magic on my Ladies' locks, and to Kat Bunker who with paint and brushes prepares their lovely faces.

Another person who deserves my gratitude is John DeStefano, who created the original mannequin, and whose company produced the bulk of the collection's figures until it closed. Since then Michael Langton Enterprises, just over the line in New Hampshire, has come to my rescue, enabling me to continue with what I refer to as "my fine madness."

Back in 1995, at the United Federation of Doll Clubs (UFDC) National Convention in Philadelphia, I had the great good fortune to meet Dr. Leonard Swann Jr., of Sirocco Productions, which led to the creation of the beautiful and imaginative Les Petites Dames de Mode video that has been enjoyed by so many of the Dames' admirers.

I should also like to express my appreciation to Nancy Rexford, a costume expert and consultant (and Danvers neighbor) who has always been available for an honest critique of my efforts.

My thanks to Mr. Robert Young for his camera expertise in photographing my demonstration of the art of packing a Lady for traveling.

To Douglas Christian—thank you for the delightful photograph of the designer, his muse and a representative gathering of the Ladies.

Special thanks to Arlene Young and Mary Eisenhauer, who examined this manuscript with sleuth-like perseverance for typographical mishaps.

Lastly, I would like to express my gratitude to the many museums that have hosted the exhibits of my Ladies, allowing their admirers to meet them in person. Through these exhibits Cile and I have had the pleasure of meeting so many delightful and interesting people, which has been perhaps the most rewarding part of this Adventure in Design.

Foreword

Since at least the 1890s, every generation has produced someone mesmerized by fashions of the past, someone who has the taste and talent to miniaturize but not minimalize modes. The current fabric bearer and magician in miniature is John Burbidge. I have long been familiar with his predecessors, and indeed have been privileged to know firsthand, and intimately, several of the groups of figures or dolls dressed in interpretations of historical fashion. All the ladies in these groups are dressed not in slavish copies but in interpretations necessitated by available materials and the artistic approach of the creator. We are talking about how an artist of one era looks at, and interprets, the fashions of another.

Long before John Burbidge's time, in 1892, in Paris an exhibition of Women's Arts was held. Among the displays was a group of dolls divided into two units: a parade of historically dressed figures and dolls in contemporary attire. These little mannequins—ordinary François Gaultier bisque-headed, leather-bodied dolls—spawned a thriving souvenir trade and had the good fortune to end up in the collection of the Musée des Arts Décoratifs, part of the great Louvre museum of France. I first encountered these marvels in the mid-1960s and revisited them in 1968.

The next groups of widely publicized and recognized fashionable historical and contemporary ladies were the work of two sisters—Mesdames Lafitte and Désirat. Fashion ran in the family; Madame Lafitte's sister-in-law was the founder of the influential French fashion magazine *Femina*. Unlike the earlier ready-made figures, these distinctive models were a result of Mesdames Lafitte and Désirat working with the wax figure makers at the Musée Grevin. Between 1908 and 1918, the crucial war year, Lafitte and Désirat turned out seasonal representations of current fashion. The early doll artist Mademoiselle E. V. Riera, who used only eight-inch-high bisque-headed figures, was inspired by paintings. While other contemporaries joined them in creating an array of widely recognized art dolls, these ladies were the leaders for the war generation.

The next group, now sadly dispersed, and known to us only from photographs, was for many years a popular feature at the Metropolitan Museum of Art in New York. Thirty-one commercial bisque-headed dolls illustrated six hundred years of fashion. They are all featured in Esther Singleton's 1927 book *Dolls*.

Then come the least remembered but most recognized figures. These are the sisters in historical dress to the now well-remembered Théâtre de la Mode mannequins. Originally forty-nine in number, these two-and-a-half-foot-high figures were created by the Syndicate de la Couture de Paris at the end of World War II. Like the contemporarily dressed figures of the Théâtre de la Mode, the historical ones have the same abstracted face and wire armature body. A particular fashion house dressed each figure. Michelle Murphy documented them in *Two Centuries of French Fashion*, a booklet published in 1949 by The Brooklyn Museum, home of these forgotten lovely ladies, where I worked for many years.

Finally, bridging the time between then and now is the work of France and Jacques Rommel, a husband-and-wife team. He created the figures and she the historical garments. Their first figure was created in 1968, and in 1979 the Fifth Avenue windows of the celebrated jeweler Cartier featured their ladies.

It was in a jeweler's windows in Princeton, New Jersey, that I first encountered the Burbidge ladies face-to-face. Since then I have watched with admiration the family of fashionables grow. It is fitting that this book preserve the dedicated delicate design work of John Burbidge, and add his name to the international constellation of stars that make the past shine for us.

—Elizabeth Ann Coleman
David and Roberta Logie Curator and Department Head, Textiles and Fashion Arts Museum of Fine Arts, Boston

Costumes are the most formal demonstration of a people's art.

ATTRIBUTED TO STEWART CULIN, MUSEUM CURATOR AND EDUCATOR, 1922

Introduction

A collection such as Les Petites Dames de Mode, or "The Ladies," as they have come to be known, is obviously not an overnight happening. Its history and story began in the 1940s, in two very different cities: Salem, Massachusetts, and Paris, France.

In the early 1940s I was a student at the New England School of Art and Design in Boston, with a vague interest in becoming a fashion designer. My knowledge was confined to textbooks so, hearing about an exhibit of period costumes at the Essex Institute in Salem, I decided to investigate it. In an upstairs gallery in this venerable building, I discovered, encased in rows of glass cases, the faded splendors of nineteenth-century haute couture. I was completely mesmerized by the intricate construction of the dresses and the incredible fabrics, colors and embroideries. In other words, I was hooked for life by the world of period costume.

This picture was taken in Paris in 1945, around the time I saw the Théâtre de la Mode.

Later, in the 1960s, I became very involved with this superb large collection, and was given the title of Honorary Curator of Costumes at the Essex. This gave me the incredible opportunity to work with these wonderful garments and to study them inside and out. Not only did this contribute much to my forty-year career as a bridal designer for the prestigious Priscilla of Boston, it also provided me with the knowledge and appreciation of period costume that would enable me to execute, with authenticity, the costumes that I now create for my Ladies.

So much for the Salem experience, and on to Paris. During my second year at art school, I became draft material and was informed that the armed services desired my presence. I shortly found myself garbed in Army fatigues (not exactly couture) with a 10th Armored Division patch on my sleeve. After a period of training, I was sent overseas, touring Europe in a tank and avoiding hostile bullets.

At the war's end I found myself billeted in a baroque castle in the heart of the Bavarian Alps, where I was to remain for several months waiting to be shipped home for discharge. Having given three years of my life to the Army and combat, going home was foremost in my mind and, despite the glamour of castle life, frustration was beginning to set in. Fortunately, the Army, in its infinite wisdom, took notice and gave us relief in the form of furloughs to Paris.

During my Army years, I had often thought of the future and had decided that the world of design was my goal. Under the assumption that this trip to Paris might be a once-in-a-lifetime event (I'm glad to say it was not), I decided to invade a few couture houses.

In those days, in Paris, an American Army uniform would open any door, and I visited several of the houses that were still in operation. It was in one of those houses that I heard about an exhibit called Théâtre de la Mode that had just opened at the Grand Gallery of the Pavilion Marsan in the Louvre. It was a group of nearly three hundred 27-inch mannequins dressed by the leading Parisian couturiers of the day, meant to show the world that, despite the war, the Paris couture was alive and well and still able to create. I recall spending hours marveling over the superb workmanship, so perfect in every detail. To create such beautiful garments in full size was impressive enough, but in that scale, it was incredible.

I often thought of those little figures over the years, and wondered what happened to them after the 1945–46 tour, which took them through Europe and to the United States, where they seemingly vanished in San Francisco. Around

1983 I read an article about a group of little fashion mannequins that had been discovered in a rather remote museum in the state of Washington, called the Maryhill Museum of Art. Lo and behold, it was the missing Théâtre de la Mode that had so captivated me in Paris in 1945. A bit the worse for wear, 150 of the remaining figures were sent back to Paris for restoration. The original stage settings had been destroyed, but were able to be reproduced. After the work was completed it was returned to the Maryhill Museum via a special exhibition at the Metropolitan Museum in New York. I attended the opening, and it was like renewing an old acquaintance that time had not changed—a real déjà vu experience.

But back to the 1940s. After the war I returned to the New England School of Art and Design, and for the next two years became a serious student of fashion design, learning to drape, make patterns, cut, sew and make up a complete garment. After graduating, I began my forty-year association with Priscilla of Boston.

By 1978 I was beginning to experience a mid-life creative crisis. By that time I had spent some thirty years working in white and ivory, with an occasional bit of pink and blue thrown in to vary the bridal palette. I began to feel like the actor who has been type cast and I wanted, if not a complete designing change, at least some more color in my life.

My interest in period costume had always stayed with me, along with the memory of those wonderful fashion dolls of the Théâtre de la Mode. The concept of the fashion doll goes back as far as the 1500s. Used as an advertising tool to show the latest style, they were highly prized and much sought-after in an age before the advent of the fashion magazine. Letters still exist from eighteenth-century ladies in the colonies to their husbands abroad, begging them to bring back a fashion doll for their dressmaker to copy. Even in the new land, with the threat of Indians on the war path, the ladies were concerned with being au courant.

Here was my solution to my mid-life creative crisis. While I continued to design for Priscilla and receive a weekly pay check, I began to visualize a series of pristine costumes on a group of perfect "Ladies," reduced to a scale wherein one could enjoy, in one sweeping glance, the varied forms of high fashion as it existed during the Victorian and Edwardian eras that I so admired. The presentation of this fashion story would require (as with the Théâtre de la Mode figures) a mannequin, as opposed to a "doll." The figure I had in mind proved rather elusive until I contacted a friend who manufactured store mannequins in fiberglass. Together we designed my idealized lady of fashion, of whom I would later write: "She is elegant, unchanging, and uncomplaining—a phantom of stylish delight that every designer would love to dress."

Chapter 1

The Design Process

The mannequin problem resolved, the costuming process began. The concept of Les Petites Dames de Mode is that I, as a contemporary designer, take myself back in time and become a Victorian or Edwardian dressmaker. Of course, the first step in that process involves extensive research. Over the years I have accumulated a large library on period costume, covering every aspect of the dress and accessories of a particular period. Having decided on a certain year in which to work, I spend hours and even days pouring through all the available information I have on that period. I study the cut of the garments, the undergarments, the prevalent colors, materials and accessories. At the same time, I turn out reams of sketches (thoughts in pencil), which help formulate the final design. I do not copy existing garments per se, but design costumes in accordance with the fashion dictates of that particular year.

The next step is the fabric choice, although sometimes a fabric that I discover sets in motion the research and sketching phase. The search for a suitable fabric often, however, raises havoc in my small workroom. My inventory has grown considerably over the years, as I have acquired the habit of picking up fabrics here, there and everywhere with a "I never know when I may need that" rationale. Based on years of research and study, I can identify the color or texture of a piece of fabric as belonging to a certain period, and the same holds true with trimmings and laces. (Flea markets are a great source for the latter two items.)

Sometimes I surrender to the beauty of a piece of antique material, knowing full well it could turn into a slippery slope. One must be very sure of the fabric's conditions, especially that which comes from pieces of old dresses. It may look good, but begin to shatter as you work with it. I find that old laces seem to age much better than fabrics, especially silk.

One of the most difficult things to achieve in creating a period costume is an authentic look. Our ancestors were not so physically different from us, but fashion has always decreed certain silhouettes to which the human body is obliged to conform. This bit of fashionable contortion in the late-nineteenth century was achieved through carefully arranged padding and a series of complicated undergarments— once modestly referred to as "unmentionables." In period dress, the unseen is the foundation for the seen, so a correctly shaped bustle, hoop or petticoat is of the utmost importance. Each mannequin wears a basic garment consisting of a corset-like bodice to be fitted against. Additional undergarments are then constructed to produce the necessary shaping for whatever period I am planning to work in.

The figure thus dressed becomes the dress form onto which I begin draping with unbleached muslin. After working out the placement of seams and lines, I transfer these muslin pieces into paper patterns. This draping process is crucial to the overall effect, such as the size and scale of a leg-of-

mutton sleeve, or the hang and drape of a skirt. It is also a vital factor when I begin to cut out the actual garment from what is usually a limited amount of fabric, which leaves no room for errors.

I use no set procedure in the construction of a costume. I may first start on either the bodice or skirt, sometimes creating as the design evolves. This happens especially when I am working in the style of the 1870s and 1880s, which involved a great deal of intricate draping effects. These were often developed directly on a foundation skirt in what the fashion writers of the time referred to as an "artistic arrangement of draperies."

I try to assemble the costumes in the same detail with which they were assembled in Victorian and Edwardian times. Bodices and skirts are lined, and often interlined. The sewing machine had become a household item during the latter half of the nineteenth century, so I machine-stitch all straight seams, while beading, trimmings and finishing are done by hand.

One of the most distinguishing features of nineteenth-century fashion was the emphasis placed on lavish and intricate trimmings. For the Victorian or Edwardian lady a "touch" of detail was not enough. Trimmings were applied by the yard. There were sumptuous embroideries and lace appliqué work, a profusion of glittering jet and shimmering encrustations of pearls, crystals and sequins. Despite the extravagant quantity of decoration, the work was done to such stunning effect that many dresses became virtual works of art in motion.

No ensemble was complete without the proper accessories, and Victorian and Edwardian wardrobes proliferated with shoes, gloves, hats, fans, parasols and jewelry. As I do not lay claim to being either a glove- or shoe-maker, I have devised certain alternative solutions. Gloves are painted on the Ladies' hands with layers of acrylic paint. For shoes, the mannequins' feet are cast in the shape of a shoe, slightly pointed and heeled. In some instances, the shoes are painted, but in most cases, I apply fabric or leather with glue to simulate the look of real shoes.

No lady would have ventured forth during the day without a hat. When these are required, I construct the shapes in buckram and wire, covering them to complement the gown. I decorate them with all the myriad trimmings that evoke the term "confections."

My Ladies represent the highest circles of society—the *beau monde*—and therefore they must not be without suitable jewels. They enjoy earrings, bracelets and necklaces of precious and semi-precious stones. One Lady carries a wonderful lorgnette in tortoise shell and sterling silver, not because of a vision problem but because it was, in those days, thought of as a smart accessory.

A pale complexion and soft hands were considered the sign of a lady of leisure; thus, a parasol was considered a vital item for any outdoor activity, as were a hat and gloves. In my wanderings through antique shops, I have discovered several scale-model parasols, which I have recovered. I also look out for parts of those

ABOVE: *Once I develop a pattern for the basic muslin, I begin to alter it, bringing it closer to the final phase, before cutting the actual costume.* RIGHT: *Any change in the pattern requires a new muslin, so it's back to the sewing machine. The fabrics I work with are limited, and I prefer to make any errors in cheap muslin.*

ubiquitous Victorian sun shades that can be recycled into miniatures. Even lovely carved handles can, with a careful wrapping of fabric, become a forgivable fake. (In a project such as this, the old adage about necessity being the mother of invention is certainly true as well as helpful.)

Also in my collection are some rare miniature fans, as well as some modern reproductions. I have three originals that I treasure, and the reproductions consist of sticks carved from wood veneer about $1/16$th of an inch thick and held together by a sterling holder or ring. They are then covered in lace or ostrich feathers. In an age devoid of air-conditioning, fans were an essential item that saved many a fair maiden from an embarrassing swoon in an overheated gas-lit ballroom.

A project as complex as Les Petites Dames de Mode cannot be measured in hours, days or even years. It is simply something that one does—for the love and joy of doing it, with no particular goal in view other than the satisfaction of personal achievement and of being able to share it with others.

I describe the mannequins as enchanting little Ladies rather than dolls to evoke their magical, "real-life" quality. Often times, when

things are not going well with a costume and nothing seems to work the way I planned, I get frustrated and lose touch with the enchantment. But then something happens to remind me that it is still there. A few years ago, a friend and a fine doll artist, Joyce Miko, wrote to me after attending one of my exhibits that: "Pictures do not begin to capture the essence of your ladies. When you see them in the 'flesh' they have about them an aura of realness, and you feel as if you are actually intruding, unseen, into a moment in each of their lives. I don't know how you did that."

I do not underestimate that old phrase, "in the eye of the beholder," and if my friend experienced something beyond the fashionable facades and elegantly expressive faces, than I can only accept her words as a most cherished compliment. They also give to my Ladies a dimension that I had not anticipated.

I must say, though, it is interesting to contemplate that these little fiberglass Ladies, while rigid of stance, have been embodied with some mysterious inner life, and that I have by my craft not only clothed them with period accuracy, but have also, in the process, somehow given them period lives as well. The Pygmalion legend revisited.

Chapter 2

Mentioning
The Unmentionables

Much interest has been expressed in the undergarments worn by Les Dames. So great is this interest that some visitors to my exhibits have actually been caught attempting to raise the Ladies' skirts to satisfy their curiosity. This breach of manners is, of course, unacceptable— not to mention the effect it has on the sensibilities of the Ladies. I have, decided, therefore, that a chapter should be devoted to the subject of the mysterious unmentionables, which hopefully shall bring a halt to these assaults on the Ladies' modesty.

For centuries the fashionable silhouette of any given period required some sort of supporting device. Hoops, bustles and paddings of all shapes, sizes and designs were used to improve the female figure divine by designers and dressmakers in order to make flesh and bone conform to fashion's latest ideal.

The fashions of the crinoline years were centered on the hoop skirt. During the 1850s skirts began to widen, requiring the support of several layers of starched petticoats. By the mid-1850s, to alleviate the weight and discomfort of the multiple petticoats, the hoop skirt was invented—or rather re-invented, as it had appeared in various forms during previous centuries as the Elizabethan farthingale and the eighteenth-century panier. This hoop structure allowed for the elimination of all the cumbersome petticoats previously worn and relied on one single petticoat to soften the hoop line.

LEFT: *This 1860s-style hoop with a cotton petticoat has a deep flounce and is bordered with cutwork embroidery from an old petticoat.* RIGHT: *An 1890s silk taffeta petticoat like this is worn underneath a ball gown with a train.*

Of course the male population laughed, cartoonists had a field day and the clergy condemned it (as they did all new fashions). As a lady walked, the swaying motion of her skirt permitted glimpses of hitherto-unseen ankles and was considered shocking. Etiquette books provided instructions on how to properly approach a chair, lest in the process of sitting one's skirt should fly up exposing goodness knows what!

High winds were treacherous, not to mention open fireplaces and rooms filled with bibelots.

However, the ladies paid little heed to all the furor for, as Doris Langley Moore remarked in her book, *The Woman in Fashion*: "The crinoline seemed absolutely indispensable to the dignity and decency of womankind. They wondered how they ever managed without it and were sure they never would again. So delusive a certainty turns every important fashion into a sort of love affair."

The hoop of the 1850s was circular, producing a dome shape, but in the 1860s it began to flatten in front, flaring out at the sides and back to assume a pyramidal shape. By the mid-1860s

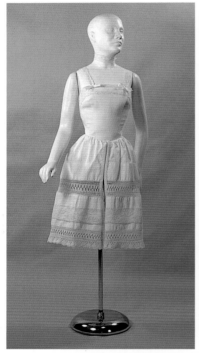

FAR LEFT: *The basic foundation worn by all mannequins is a combination of a fitted bodice and knee-length drawers. The bodice section softens the fiberglass body, helping to fit and shape the costumes. Sometimes these are used as separate pieces.*
LEFT: *A "hip improver" has been added to the basic foundation. Throughout all of these periods a well-rounded figure was the ideal. I find the hip improver very useful in adjusting the shape and hang of the skirt.*

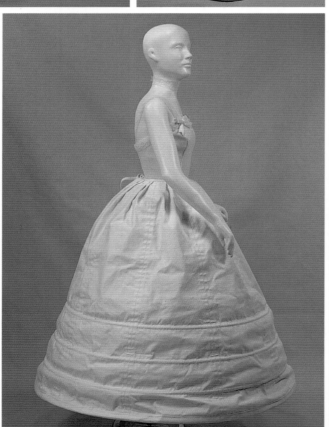

OPPOSITE PAGE, FAR LEFT: *An 1850s-style hoop of polished cotton has rings of plastic boning set in casings made from cotton bias tape.* **OPPOSITE PAGE, LEFT:** *In the late 1860s and early 1870s the crinolette came into vogue.* **ABOVE, LEFT:** *The 1860s-style hoop of polished cotton also has plastic boning set in casings of bias cotton tape, but the shape is more pyramidal.* **LEFT:** *This was one of the basic bustle shapes of the 1870s.* **ABOVE:** *This 1850s-style hoop has a cotton petticoat. The flounce has several rows of tucking and a lace edge.*

ABOVE, LEFT: *Padding and other complex feats of engineering made a variety of bustle shapes possible in the 1870s and 1880s.* LEFT: *I use this kind of bustle support for the mid- and late-1880s clothing.* ABOVE: *This silk satin petticoat is in the 1895 style.* OPPOSITE PAGE, RIGHT: *By 1900, the silk taffeta petticoats have a slimmer, more flaring shape.* OPPOSITE PAGE, FAR RIGHT: *The new style of narrow gowns of the 1900–1914 era require narrow petticoats such as these.*

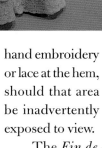

it obtained its greatest circumference and began to reduce in size, evolving into the crinolette, with emphasis concentrated at the back. This shape lent support to a new fashion about to appear, which would become known as the bustle.

The bustle style appeared in the very early 1870s and continued on in various forms until its demise at the very end of the 1880s. All sorts of supporting shapes were devised for this unique phase in the history of fashion, from complex feats of engineering to simple padding. The term "bustle" was considered by some a bit common, whereas *tournure* or "back projection" was thought to be more refined. Regardless of terminology, the media had a field day.

By the end of the 1880s the back projections had been reduced to a simple bit of fullness, and all the intricate bustle supports were relegated to trunks in the attic. Fashion in the 1890s focused attention on huge sleeves, wasp waists and sweeping circular skirts, and the petticoat came "out of the closet" (to use a contemporary phrase)!

The petticoats of the proper Victorian era had been functional and utilitarian and were meant to be invisible. They were made of washable cottons, linen or occasionally silk, with touches of delicate

hand embroidery or lace at the hem, should that area be inadvertently exposed to view.

The *Fin de Siècle* (end of the century) was the beginning of the Edwardian Age, which evolved into *La Belle Epoque* (the beautiful era) and vanished with the outbreak of World War I. Ostentatious display was in; Victorian propriety was out, and the seductive rustle of taffeta petticoats was heard throughout the land. Yards and yards of silken flounces were trimmed with yards and yards of ribbons and lace, and those ubiquitous etiquette books advised on the proper way for a lady to hold her skirts in order to show a glimpse of those wondrous undergarments, which was guaranteed to drive men mad. (How times had changed!)

To construct the undergarments necessary to produce the proper silhouette for the various costumes, I have studied period examples. The samples shown here are based on this research and adapted to the size and scale of my mannequins.

Chapter 3

The Crinoline Years 1855–1869

The Petites Dames collection begins in the mid-nineteenth century with the introduction around 1856 of the "steel cage," or hoopskirt. It is said to have been the brainchild of a clever Frenchman (there is always someone coming up with a better mousetrap!), but regardless of origin, the ladies took to this new invention with great joy and relief, being finally freed from their suffocating layers of petticoats.

The first "cage" in 1856 was round, producing a dome shape that allowed the fabric to fall in pleasing folds. This changed into a pyramidal shape, with a flattened front and flaring at the sides and back, in the 1860s. By 1865–1866 skirts had ballooned to their fullest width. By that time, as happens with every fashion, a new trend was developing (the first having been wrung dry of ideas) and the Age of the Crinoline's mergence with the Age of the Bustle was beginning.

However, between these two modes, the dressmakers worked their magic, with that arch-creator Charles Frederick Worth as head wizard. His dresses for the Empress Eugenie, who discovered him, launched him on the road to fame and fortune. The House of Worth became the couture temple of worship for everyone from queens to ladies of the demimonde, and all those in between who wished to be part of the fashionable world.

Despite the nasty pens of the cartoonists, the scathing sermons of the clergy, being a fire hazard, monopolizing space, being difficult to manage and an all-around inconvenience—despite all this, the crinoline mode was without doubt one of fashion's loveliest moments. In portraits by Winterhalter the ladies appear with ethereal charm in clouds of tulle and shimmering fabrics, and his great painting of the Empress Eugenie and her ladies-in-waiting evokes all the grace and elegance of this enchanting fashion.

It was a style flattering to many (although there is always a frog among the swans) with the fitted bodice and pointed or round waist made illusively smaller by billowing skirts. It is interesting to note that 150 years later, this styling is still a design inspiration for that most romantic of costumes, the bridal gown, and I'm sure that variations will continue to move majestically down church aisles for years to come.

Plate 1

Afternoon Costume circa 1856

A structure with rings of wire or whalebone and called a "cage" or "crinoline" or "hoop" appeared around the mid-1850s to replace the multiple petticoats necessary to support the ever-widening skirts. Completely circular in shape, it caused the skirt, which flowed over it, to assume an attractive dome shape, which was the fashionable silhouette of the 1850s.

For this Afternoon Costume, I incorporated several style features of the mid-1850s—a basque or jacket bodice, V-shaped bodice trim, pagoda or funnel sleeves and a flounced skirt.

A blue silk taffeta was my choice of color and fabric, with trim of black velvet ribbon and lace. The skirt is comprised of three graduated flounces accented with the trim and edged with a row of self-fabric fringe.

The V-shaped bodice trim is highlighted by three strategically placed pale-blue silk ribbon bows. From beneath the funnel-shaped sleeves appear fine white

linen and lace under-sleeves, known as *engageantes*, usually worn with this type of sleeve. Black jet buttons secure the front opening, and the costume is accessorized with gold earrings, a gold locket and a chatelaine of gold-colored metal from which is suspended a pair of scissors. (Madame's fingers are not idle.)

In addition to the proper hoop, and a lace-trimmed petticoat of polished cotton, the Lady wears a pair of black-trimmed blue boots (in this case painted). I have also provided her with a pair of long drawers should an accidental "hoop upheaval" cause her limbs to be exposed.

This "trembling and gyrating dome," with its extravagant consumption of fabric, required a skilled navigator to maneuver about the overcrowded decor of a typical Victorian drawing room—not to mention the possibility of instant incineration from flying fireplace sparks. However, the lure and glamour of high fashion made these inconveniences a matter of minor consideration.

Plate 2

Evening Costume circa 1856

From 1852 to 1870 the Second French Empire reigned in splendor and extravagance, and Paris was the undisputed epicenter of the fashionable world. The society ladies on both sides of the Atlantic (as well as those of easy virtue known as the demimonde), flocked to the Paris dressmakers to order lavish wardrobes—a Paris dress being their social security blanket.

The inspiration for this Evening Costume was a delicate cream-colored Chantilly lace patterned with swirling scrolls and flowers. A length of pale-mauve silk resting in my to-be-used-some-day fabric collection seemed to be the perfect background for the lace. While wandering through the artificial-flower section of a local craft store, I spotted sprays of mauve and cream flowers. These, applied by hand with mauve and crystal beads, are the special ingredients that achieve the successful combination of beautiful and expensive.

Victorian modesty required a complete covering during the day. Exposed shoulders and arms that would have shocked in daytime hours, however, were quite acceptable during the evening. This bodice is cut with a point in front and back; a bertha of antique Brussels lace edged in silk tulle and garlands of flowers outlines the low-cut neckline. Bows of mauve silk accent the shoulders, each with a "jeweled" center of mauve beads.

Madame's hair is center-parted and pulled back into a chignon, adorned with a wreath of beaded silk flowers. Drops of amethyst crystal encircle her neck on a violet velvet ribbon with matching drop earrings. She wears bracelets of pearl and amethyst, and carries a mauve silk fan edged in sequined lace, should the overheated ballroom cause discomfort. Her dancing slippers are of ivory silk satin with mauve silk bows.

We hope that, so gowned, Madame has been able to put her vanity at ease, and at the same time been able to acquire the favorable opinion of *La Vie Parisienne*.

Three or four trimmings were not enough for a simple dress; when it had lace and garlands of flowers, ribbons and frills, they put a jewel in the center of every bow. And then it was that woman was able to satisfy one of her vanities: she could display a dress not just because it was beautiful, but because it was expensive, too.

La Vie Parisienne
JOANNA RICHARDSON

Plate 3

Day Costume circa 1858

*A*ll dresses of the late 1850s were not as exuberant of design as the flounced gown in Plate 1. Many, although conforming to the fashion of the period and being of rich fabric, were of a simpler construction and detailing.

To create this quietly elegant Day Costume, suitable for visiting or other daytime activity, I found, in a fabric shop in New York, a beautiful silk faille material, which had been woven in Italy specifically for men's neckties. It is of a stripe design in shades of deep plum, combined with narrow bands of silvery green, beige and black.

As was the custom at this period, the skirt is cut in rectangular-shaped panels, which require the absorbing of a great deal of material into the waistband. This I accomplished by a large amount of pleating, thus creating a domed, or bell-shaped, skirt.

The bodice conforms to the popular V-shape attained by cutting the fabric on the bias. It dips to a point in the front and to a very deep one in back. The sleeves are of the wide pagoda cut, with cream-colored lace under-sleeves, which match the collar.

Both of these items were usually removable from the dress for laundering. A shaped bertha of fine black lace and satin ribbon emphasizes the sloping-shoulder look that was considered so ladylike at the time.

While working on this costume, I found in my inventory of bits and pieces a length of delicate braid that matched the green in the fabric. I used this as a trim to accent various details on the bodice. Several rows also appear on the skirt and create a sort of faux flounce effect.

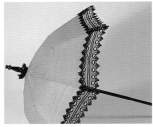

I have provided the Lady with a suitable bonnet for venturing outdoors. It is of lilac silk trimmed with antique cream lace, black lace and cream tulle with ties of lilac silk. Her earrings are tiny oval cameos set in gold, and her boots are of black silk and grosgrain. The indispensable parasol is covered in green silk.

I trust that Mr. Wells would find this dress in keeping with his dictum, and that my Lady may face the fashionable world secure and confident in her choice of toilette.

Plate 4

Ball Gown circa 1863

As I have chosen to concentrate on the haute-couture fashions of the periods, my research includes various publications that record the lifestyle and customs (not to mention gossip) of its high society. The quote about the first ball at the Tuileries from Mrs. Moulton's recollections became the inspiration for this 1863 Ball Gown.

It was customary to appear in one's wedding gown at the first ball one attended as a married lady. Lillie Moulton, a lady of wealth and great musical talent, who moved in very exalted circles and was well-versed in the social mores, would have known that her wedding gown was the proper attire for the occasion. According to her memoir, her first appearance was a great success, and she became a popular figure at the imperial court.

With Mrs. Moulton's "wedding dress, trimmed with beautiful lace" in mind, I settled on a piece of fine antique net appliquéd with flowers and leaves and lacy ribbon-like motifs that had seen better days and which, I felt, deserved a fashion rebirth.

Using an 1860s-style hoop, with its flaring pyramidal shape, I was able to drape a full-trained skirt of silk taffeta as a foundation for the new life of the appliquéd net. The effect was exactly what I wanted—an elegant opulence suitable for a grand society wedding or an imperial ball!

The bodice is cut from the same silk taffeta, with a deep pointed waist. Short puffed sleeves with a just-off-the-shoulder neckline appear to have been the uniform cut for ball gowns of the period. Bows of satin ribbon frame the shoulders. A V-shaped plastron of net and appliquéd lace embroidered with pearls and crystals emphasizes the pointed bodice line. A similar arrangement is used on the back bodice.

Over the voluminous folds at the back of the skirt lays a double sash of satin ribbon caught together, two-thirds of the way down, by a large bow. The ends of the sash continue on to the hem of the train.

Madame's hair is dressed with an arrangement of satin ribbons entwined with pearls. A triple-strand pearl necklace and pearl earrings are her only jewels. The indispensable fan is of lace, and her shoes of ivory silk satin.

I like to think of Mrs. Moulton moving through the dazzling splendors of the Tuileries palace in a gown such as this, for as she wrote: "The beautifully dressed ladies were covered with jewels, and the gentlemen in their showy uniforms were covered with decorations. Each lady showed to great advantage, as, on account of the width of their crinolines, they had to stand very far apart. It was a magnificent sight, and as long as I live I shall never forget It."

Dear M., We received the invitation for the first ball at the Tuileries... my wedding dress, trimmed with beautiful lace, seemed the proper thing to wear.

In the Courts of Memory
Mrs. Charles Moulton
née Lillie De Hegermann-Lindencrone

Plate 5

Carriage Toilette circa 1865

To live in this perfect place and be a member of high society was a constant struggle, but a burden to be borne. There were endless rules and rituals to be observed, and a fall from grace was not to be tolerated.

One of these rituals was the Lady's afternoon carriage drive, presumably to enjoy the fresh air, but far more important, to be seen, and to display her affluent position in the scheme of things. In addition to a beautiful carriage, a pair of fine horses, a handsome coachman and an equally dashing footman in full livery, Madame must be elegantly gowned. According to the publication *Manners, Culture, and Dress of the Best American Society* by Richard A. Wells, a lady was advised that her toilette "for a drive through the streets of a city or along a fashionable drive or park can not be too rich in material. Silks, velvets and laces are all appropriate, with rich jewelry and costly furs."

Accordingly, for this Carriage Toilette I chose a brilliant green silk, similar to one of those vibrant shades attained by the use of aniline dyes that were much admired in the 1860s. Actually, this particular shade of green had a drawback, for one of the chemicals used in its production was arsenic. It is recorded that a young girl who went to a ball wearing a green dress succumbed to an illness caused by the dye, and died after an evening's dancing. (*Victorian and Edwardian Fashion: A Photographic Study* by Alison Gernsheim) Literally a fashion to die for!

The bodice has a natural waist, and the sleeves are cut in the two-piece coat style with elbow fullness. Black velvet ribbon combined with black lace creates a squared yoke effect and extends to the back in a deep V-shape. Tiny jet buttons accent the front opening, and a wide black velvet belt encircles the waist, ending in the back with two fringed bows of green silk.

The skirt is made up of eight panels; the center front and center back panels are cut on the fold. Each skirt seam terminates at the hem with a single loop bow with two long fringed ends, the bow loop and ends caught together with green and jet beads. The hem is bound in black velvet ribbon.

The design of the dress is elegantly simple, but the sumptuousness of the total costume is achieved by the protectively inadequate, but extravagantly beautiful, black

Chantilly-lace coat. This is made from one of those large triangular lace shawls of the 1860s that seem to proliferate at antique shows and shops dealing in period costumes. After some skillful mending, I managed to fashion the shawl into a flowing mantle with wide set-in sleeves. The front opening is held in place by satin bows, and a tracery of jet beads outlines the front closure and the scallop detail on the sleeve and coat borders.

A bonnet of green silk trimmed in black lace and cream silk tulle with pink ties nearly completes the Toilette—but no lady could venture out sans her parasol. For this one I altered an actual Victorian sunshade and covered it to match the ensemble.

And so, with parasol held aloft, its fringe fluttering in the breeze, moving slowly along the sun-dappled avenues of the Bois de Boulogne in her splendid equipage, the Lady can acknowledge and observe acquaintances turned out in equal splendor, participating in the same ritual, secure in the knowledge that they are keeping up appearances, and that all is well in *their* world.

Plate 6

Afternoon Dress circa 1865

Being a lady in the Victorian period seems to have been a demanding and all-consuming occupation. If one had not been born to the aristocracy, like Grace Vanderbilt, and grown up accustomed to her world of gentility, there was an endless supply of publications available to guide one along the slippery slope leading to that pinnacle of social acceptance. There was of course much emphasis on matters pertaining to dress. In *Manners, Culture, and Dress of the Best American Society* the following admonition was made: "Numbers have owed their elevation to their attention to the toilette. Place, fortune, marriage have all been lost by neglecting it." Food for thought indeed!

This demure and restrained Afternoon Dress would certainly have been considered very proper and ladylike, assuring all that its wearer was of the genteel class, and not about to sully her hands with any menial tasks. Pale-grey silk with trim of lapis-blue silk fringe seemed to be a suitable choice for a leisurely afternoon of ladylike activities: needlework, letter writing, reading (something instructional or poetry) or painting in watercolors (flowers and fruit acceptable). A band of grey silk edged with fringe and grey braid encircle the upper bodice. Old lace forms a collar at the high

neck and sleeve cuffs, and steel-cut buttons accent the front closing. The waist is girdled by a pointed belt of the grey silk and closes at the back with a bow and wide flaring streamers finished in the blue fringe.

The trained skirt is bordered with a silk band trimmed with grey braid and blue fringe over a pleated flounce of grey silk. Boots are of grey velveteen.

The Lady's jewelry consists of lapis earrings and a gold brooch, which contains a lock of hair that I found on one of my antique-shop excursions. The lock of hair probably belongs to a family member (unless the Lady has a secret I am not aware of!).

Attired thus, Madame could relax in the knowledge that she has properly attended to her toilette, and that her place, fortune and marriage are secure. Although all this striving for perfection could bring on a migraine or a case of the vapors, such a malady could be relieved by a sip of "medicinal" sherry.

Plate 7

Ball Gown circa 1866

It was a fashion suitable for those who were young, graceful, and wealthy, who had carriages to ride in, large houses or palaces to live in, immense storage cupboards, and little or nothing to do.

The Age of Worth
EDITH SAUNDERS

Edith Saunders is referring to the crinoline, and the privileged members of society who were the only ones entitled to wear it. Like all fashion innovations, though first worn by the fashionable avant-garde, it soon filtered down to the hoi polloi. Even domestics appeared in crinolines—to the consternation of their employers, who were always on the alert to keep everyone in their place.

By the mid-1860s the crinoline had reached its apogee, and was beginning its descent into fashion history. Fashions do not disappear overnight, however, and the gored skirts, fitted at the waist with gathers confined to the back, required support for the wide sweeping skirt.

Considering the volume of these 1860s skirts, much ingenuity on the part of the dressmakers was required to decorate the surfaces. The skirt was like a vast canvas awaiting the artist's brush.

For this Ball Gown I decided on a dramatic combination of black and white, a color scheme much used during this period. For the basic gown I used a lustrous Italian silk, and for the decoration, two pieces of beautiful black nineteenth-century lace. Of the wider border piece there was just enough to ease around the bottom of the skirt, which displays the beautiful floral pattern of the lace. It is secured to the skirt with a bias cut, serpentine-like ruching of the white silk, caught at intervals with silk bows. A band of the same ruching appears under the lace at the hemline.

The skirt is cut in several fitted gores; the only gathering is confined to the center back panels. Each of these back panels is highlighted by narrow lace panels, which are joined to the lace border by large white silk bows with self-fringed ends. The bodice has a round waist, slightly raised, with the usual off-the-shoulder neckline, trimmed with the serpentine ruching and black lace, short sleeves and a self-fabric belt, closing at the back with a large bow.

The headpiece is of purple velvet flowers and ribbons, and the jewelry is of amethyst and pearls. The fan is of black lace suspended on a purple satin ribbon. The shoes are white satin.

In *The Age of Worth*, it is written that the fashion of the crinoline was "fantastic and absurd, as well as inconvenient and uncomfortable," and yet, on the other hand, "the ladies of fashion glide about with an unearthly charm, romantic and unapproachable." Charming and romantic, yes. But judging from all recorded scandals of the period, the term "unapproachable" is questionable.

Still, the reign of the crinoline was indeed one of fashion's most beguiling interludes, and the Paris of the Second French Empire, with all its extravagance and gaiety, its perfect setting. The ladies were in love with the crinoline, declared it indispensable and would never part with it—until, that is, a new fashion appeared and the indispensable (along with the Empire) became only a memory.

Chapter 4

The Reign of the Bustle 1870-1889

From 1870 until the closing years of the 1880s the focus of fashion was on that area of the anatomy charmingly referred to in French as *la derrière*. In the late 1860s, having exhausted all possible decorative variations on the crinoline style, as well as sensing client ennui, designers began exploring back interest. At the same time, ladies were becoming more active out of doors and the game of croquet was considered a suitable sport for the fair sex. Long, full and trailing skirts, however, were as much a problem for such an activity as they were for a stroll in the park. Creative minds quickly resolved the problem by looping up the skirts by a series of either concealed buttons or tapes. This of course allowed a slight display of petticoat and high-buttoned boots, causing alarm among the fashion vigilantes—another tempest in the teapot of fashion

This practical solution to a perplexing problem soon developed into the first bustle phase. The raised skirt became the tunic-like polonaise overskirt, gathered up at the back by a series of tape-controlled soft puffs, while the petticoat became the underskirt, both decorated with a profusion of flounces, lace, ribbons, flowers and anything else the dressmakers could find room for.

By 1875 phase two began with the elongation of the bodice, which descended revealingly over the hips. The skirts became sheath-like, with complex draping terminating in trains, even for day wear. By 1878 the tightly fitting bodice and skirt became one and was called the princess dress, allegedly in honor of the beautiful Alexandra, Princess of Wales. Around 1883, the back projection began its final fling, reaching its greatest size by mid-decade.

It must be said that the Bustle Epoch was not flattering for all. But for the tall or well-proportioned, the fashion clothed the wearer with a regal distinction, despite the restrictive construction and complex design of these ornate costumes. The art of sitting required a certain dexterity in the management of so much fabric (not to mention the bustle support itself), but the ladies' magazines offered guidance on how to arrange one's self, and draperies, with utmost assurance and dignity.

In 1889 the bustle was but a whisper of its former self, a mere pad to support the rather un-inspirational silhouette typical of the transitional lull that sometimes exists between two dramatic modes. However, lurking in the late 1880s bodice is the hint of things to come—a raised, gathered sleeve cap which will become the fabled leg-of-mutton sleeve of the Fin de Siècle.

Plate 8

Promenade Toilette circa 1870

As is the case with any innovative fashion, damnation is guaranteed, regardless of its practicality or beauty. Considering those unmanageable trailing skirts of the 1860s, the sanitary aspect of a short skirt (even if only a few inches off the ground) had great merit. Its first wearers, however, were condemned as "fast," until the Empress Eugenie appeared in a walking skirt, for her approval was enough to popularize any fashion.

Short walking dresses began appearing in the fashion plates of *Harper's Bazar* in the late 1860s and early 1870s, and this Promenade Toilette is an example of their elaborate design. Two tones of pale-blue *peau de soie* and black lace were my choice of color and fabric. The garment is comprised of four pieces: bodice, overskirt, underskirt and belt with attached panels. The bodice is cut in the round-waist style, with a V-shaped neckline framed in a fichu of silk fringe, braid and black lace. The sleeves are finished with the same fringe, braid and black lace.

A belt of black velvet ribbon encircles the waist. At the back, suspended from the belt, are two elaborate panels of silk in cascading folds, trimmed in black lace and velvet ribbon.

The overskirt gores are cut in points, each seam outlined in narrow black lace. The points are bound with the deeper blue *peau de soie*, outlined with braid, edged in self-fringe and accented with bows of the deeper blue silk.

The underskirt of black Chantilly lace over pale-blue silk, with a flounce trimmed in braid and self-fringe, is reminiscent of elaborate eighteenth-century petticoats. Actually the braid that appears on various parts of this costume is hairpin lace. It was made many years ago by my wife Cile (she-who-never-throws-anything-away). It sat around all this time waiting for the right moment. This Petite Dame's gown seemed to provide that right moment, and Cile graciously donated it to the cause.

For the boots I decided to use the hand-painted method. At a wonderful exhibit at the Museum of Fine Arts in Boston in 1963 I noticed that one of the mannequins had painted-on boots. I thought this a great solution to the shoe problem—a piece of information I recalled when faced with the same difficulty with my Ladies.

The hat also follows the new back-interest trend. A buckram-and-wire shape with a high crown and rolled brim is covered in blue silk with a cluster of velvet ribbons, black lace and silk bows at the back. With the hair piled high in elaborate twists and curls, the hat sits fashionably forward, secured by lethal hatpins.

In her book *Victorian and Edwardian Fashion: A Photographic Study*, Alison Gernsheim wrote: "The puff at the rear which was an outstanding feature of the early seventies had already begun to make its appearance in 1868, when Paris decreed that there shall be an abundance of crinoline, or bustle, or panier, or *tournure* (for the bunch at the back goes by a variety of names) just below the waist." Paris decreed, the ladies obeyed, and the bustle in its various permutations would be the fashionable silhouette for the next two decades.

Influenced probably by the extravagant and artificial Second Empire, a more sophisticated type of girl appeared in the late sixties than any during the previous thirty years. High heels (at the most 1¹/₂"), short skirts (ending just above the ankle), chignons of extra hair, make-up, and other adjuncts of beauty, were abominated by the admirers of the gentle, drooping womanhood of the forties and fifties.

Victorian and Edwardian Fashion: A Photographic Study
ALISON GERNSHEIM

Plate 9

Toilette de Bal circa 1870

I would like to assure my readers that, in choosing this elegant orange color for the Toilette de Bal, I in no way meant to cast aspersions on the purity of my Ladies, and that consideration of animal or any other kind of passion would be beneath their notice.

Actually the use of this vibrant shade presented me with a bit of a problem. I was not sure in which period this color would have been popular, but, as luck would have it, I had among my research material a series of Costume Calendars published by the Costume Society of America. In the 1998 edition (Reflections in Time), in the month of September, is shown a stunning evening dress in brilliant orange silk taffeta, circa 1868–69, from the collection at the McCord Museum in Montreal.

The color problem resolved, I moved ahead with the design of the dress, which is a combination of silk taffeta and silk satin. The taffeta is used for the bodice and tunic style overskirt, and the satin for the underskirt, puff trim and bows. (The puffs are made from lengths of bias strips, the edges folded in and caught together at intervals).

The draped silk taffeta overskirt is edged in puffs and bows of silk satin. Both the puffs and bows are "knotted" with twists of coral-colored pearls and crystal beads. The beads are sewn on with orange threads, which turn the clear crystal a soft coral shade. Two flounces of delicate cream-colored lace are arranged over the orange silk satin underskirt, with a heading of satin puffs.

The silk taffeta bodice is natural-waisted, and has a shaped belt of silk satin. The off-the-shoulder neckline is set off by a bertha of lace and silk tulle. The lace is embellished with a beading of the coral-colored pearls and crystal. Puffs of the satin circle the bertha, and there are satin bows at each shoulder. Small puffed sleeves of silk taffeta are barely visible beneath the bertha.

The Toilette is completed with a diadem of pearl and coral flowers in the Russian *kokosnik* fashion, with a necklace, earrings and bracelets of pearl and coral. Her shoes are orange silk satin.

A gown such as this would not be for the timid, but for the self-assured lady whose entrance into a gas-lit (a flattering light for this color) ballroom would have caused a flutter of fans and a rustle of whispers. The gentlemen would have greatly admired this striking titian-haired beauty (no doubt the ladies less so), her dance card would have been full, and her evening a grand success.

Afternoon Costume circa 1872

By the conclusion of the 1860's, the fashionable silhouette had changed dramatically. The circular volume of the skirt no longer centered on the wearer, but sailed out behind her. Readers of The Englishwomen's Domestic Magazine were advised to take their long gored skirts and 'arrange' it to the present fashionable style by gathering it up at the sides and back so as to form a large puff.

Simply Stunning
CHARLES OTTO THIEME

This Afternoon Costume could be considered an example of the transitional process of one fashion into another, which is rarely, if ever, an overnight event. The very term "fashion" implies something transitory. Jean Cocteau defined it nicely when he said: "One must forgive fashion everything—it dies so young!"

Toward the end of the 1860s the crinoline was deflating and skirt interest was focusing on the back. In order for ladies to move about out of doors with a bit more comfort, the long trailing skirts were being outfitted with a series of cords and tapes and rings sewn on the inside of the skirt. This caused the skirt to be looped up in attractive swags exposing a decorative petticoat, and allowed for much easier walking. Soon the looped-up-skirt became the polonaise drape and the ladies of the haut monde were transformed into nineteenth-century versions of eighteenth-century shepherdesses—sans sheep.

The design of the Afternoon Costume is very eighteenth century in mood, the dresses of this period being inspired by those of the latter years of the ancien régime. A crisp silk taffeta in stripes of pale-green and cream seemed an appropriate choice, with a deeper green for the trim. A crinolette with a bustle "pad" and petticoat supports the skirt, which is comprised of two pieces—a polonaise-style overskirt and a petticoat underskirt. The puffs of the back drape are controlled by a series of tapes, which, if untied, allow the section to lay out flat (making for easy pressing and packing). Both of these sections are edged with pleated flounces finished with a heading of bias puffings laid on a band of cream-colored lace. Bows join the two sections at the side.

The bodice is cut in the round-waist style, with a square neckline outlined with pleated taffeta, puffings and lace, and a fringed bow at the center front. The long sleeves are finished in the same manner. Tiny buttons covered in cream-colored silk satin appear on the front closure, and the belt is of the striped taffeta cut on the cross. The jewelry consists of earrings made from a pair of steel-cut buttons, and a marquisite butterfly at the neck of the lace inset.

The hat is covered in the silk taffeta with a smart rolled brim of cream lace over taffeta and filled with silk flowers in pale pinks, yellows and lilacs. There are long trailing velvet streamers, quaintly referred to as "follow-me-boys." The parasol is of matching silk, with an off-white wooden handle.

In October 1995, when I lectured for the Michigan Doll Makers Guild, member Monica Pendygraft told me she was to have her long hair cut and wanted to send me the cutting to make a wig for one of my Ladies. A lady's lock of hair is a very romantic gesture—but I was offered the whole thing! Monica's "lock of hair" has become this Lady's crowning glory.

Many of the dresses of the period were designed with additional pieces that change the costume to suit a different occasion. On this dress, the removal (with the assistance of a maid) of the lace chemisette reveals a square open neckline that transforms it into a dinner or informal evening gown.

The crinoline to which the ladies had pledged their undying allegiance was now demodé, and the dresses it had supported were being arranged to the puff of the bustle. But fashion has an interesting revival rate. In 1947 a man by the name of Christian Dior rocked the fashion world with the New Look and the Crinoline Look was back.

Plate 11

Ball Gown circa 1873

*I*n days of yore the rules of etiquette left nothing to chance, and there was always help available for those unfortunates who found themselves in the unenviable situation of being part of the décor.

The composition of this costume harks back to the rococo period of Louis XV— a reference that appealed to the aspirations of many of those moving up the ladder from lesser positions in the social pecking order. My selection of fabrics for this Ball Gown was silk taffeta and silk satin in matching shades of pink, and for trim, crystal-beaded lace combined with velvet and fabric flowers. The design of the bodice incorporates a fichu-style neckline, which the fashion writers of the day invariably associated with the ill-fated Marie Antoinette. It is of lace over satin with crystal embroidery, and garlanded with flowers.

The silk satin apron-style overskirt, with a deep border of flowers, lace and crystal, sweeps back into a large satin pouf, which is caught together by a satin-bound silk taffeta bow with pointed streamers strewn with lace and flowers. Beneath the bow is a fan-shaped section; from underneath falls a satin train.

Both of these sections are finished with deep borders of beaded lace, flowers and silk tulle pleating. It can be said that in the early 1870s too much was never enough! The underskirt consists of shirred bands of silk taffeta alternating with bands of silk satin—rather plain compared with the rest of the dress.

The lady's coiffure is dressed with pink flowers, and her earrings are crystal

drops. For her neck treatment, I recalled a lovely painting by Tissot entitled *Too Early* (1873), depicting a group of ladies and gentlemen who have arrived at the ball prematurely. Each of the ladies wears a ribbon around her neck with long trailing streamers. Thank you, Monsieur Tissot, for your assistance!

The fan shown with this costume is of special interest. It is a fine antique piece of hand-painted ivory. During a trip to Paris, my wife and I were wandering through the city's famous flea market and, always on the look out for items for the collection, I spotted two lovely miniature fans. I knew that they were meant for my Ladies. (The second one can be seen in Plate 14).

I am confident that my Lady in pink will not require the intervention of the master of the house to extricate her from a wallflower position. Without doubt she will leave the ball with her self-esteem quite intact, if not happily exhausted from having danced all night.

Plate 12

Visiting Costume circa 1875

*A*s the call of ceremony should last no longer than fifteen minutes, a lady would enter the drawing room, greet her hostess, engage in a bit of small talk and depart, leaving the proscribed number of calling cards, to repeat the same performance at her next stop.

The design of this Visiting Costume is an example of the complicated construction of the bustle style that began emerging during the 1870s, and that would continue on throughout the 1880s. By 1875 the puffy softness of the early 1870s had disappeared and the bodice had begun its descent toward the hipline, the skirt had tightened across the front, and all interest was now centered on the rear of the dress.

In designing this gown I utilized a dress of the period, which had been a gift from a local family. Although aware of the treacherous nature of period fabrics, I decided to take my chances. What appealed to me was the combination of fabrics, a plain silk taffeta and a figured damask, the taffeta in a shade of olive-green and the damask in a rich blend of olive and cream, all very much in keeping with the period.

The bodice is of the new cuirass style, which tightly enveloped the figure down to the hipline, in the manner of a suit of armor, from which the term cuirass comes. Following a fashion feature of the day, the bodice incorporates both fabrics, using a plastron of the plain silk in the front and back, with gored sides in the damask. The sleeves are of the plain silk with flaring cuffs of pleating and lace.

There is a standing collar of the plain silk and lace, with an inner wing collar and bow of organdy. Down the center of the front plastron is an arrangement of lace and gold buttons, which conceals the opening. The back plastron ends in a large decorative bow trimmed with lace and fringe. The hem of the bodice is finished with two narrow folds—one of the plain olive silk, the other of a pale-gold satin.

The draped damask skirt is arranged over a basic foundation to which the various folds are tacked into position. The back skirt is cut in several gores that fan out into a peacock train with a complex arrangement of damask and plain silk drapery, lace, tassels and fringe. The bottom of the skirt is bordered with a deep pleating of the plain silk (from the original dress) over which is laid a length of corded and tasseled fringe (also from the original dress). Attached to the under-hem is a frill of lace called a *balayeuse*, or "sweeper." These are found under all trained dresses of the Victorian and Edwardian period, and were used to keep the hem of the skirts clean.

One of those little fashion oddities appeared at this time in the form of an ornamental pocket, impractically placed low at the back of the skirt. The one that appears here was the actual watch pocket from the original dress, which I further embellished with a bow and clusters of tassels.

Accessories for this costume include one of the tiny hats of the period. Also, as this is intended to be a fall toilette, I decided to provide the Lady with a "finger-warming muff."

Although exceedingly restrictive and cumbersome to manage, the Lady's costume for this important function would have been worth the effort. Having been duly noticed by all, she could now return home secure in the knowledge that she had properly executed one of the rituals necessitated by her position in society.

The censorious Thorstein Veblen may have referred to paying calls as 'purposeless leisure', but the call of ceremony was the basic unit of social intercourse. It was how a lady made acquaintances, who in turn became friends. At its most purely ceremonial, it was something to get dressed up for.

To Marry an English Lord
CAROL MCD.WALLACE & GAIL MCCOLL

Plate 13

Princess Reception Dress circa 1878

Nothing can be a more certain indication that the wearer of a long train is not a lady, than the fact that she allows it to sweep the street behind her.

Dress-Art At Home Series 1878
Margaret Oliphant

The fashions of the late 1870s seem to have been intentionally designed for the sole purpose of separating the social chaff from the wheat. Wealth, leisure and position notwithstanding, the princess sheath dress, with its confining fit and encumbering sash-like draperies, tended to reduce a lady's mobility to a snail's pace. Its long spreading train was virtually impossible to pick up with any degree of dignity. The entire concept intimated that the wearer was of the carriage class and, therefore, a lady.

I decided that a length of multi-colored striped silk would work well with the elongated princess lines and, to go with it, I selected a deep-grey silk taffeta that matched one of the stripes. The dress is composed of twelve slim gores, eight being of the stripe and four of the grey silk (used in the center front and center back). By very careful placement of the pattern pieces on the stripe, the seams are almost invisible. At the center back the two grey gores terminate approximately halfway down the back, where they join four flaring panels of the striped silk to form a long fan-shaped train. The train is lined with a layer of black net and a deep facing of grey silk.

The entire center front of the gown is a long panel composed of rows of pleated grey silk alternating with fringed "fans" of the same silk. A jabot of bows and draped

silk conceals the front opening. Black braid frames both the front and back panels, and extends around the entire skirt just above a pleated flounce of the grey silk taffeta.

The long fitted sleeves are finished with fine black lace and braid, and grey silk bows. A dramatic two-piece sash of wide black silk taffeta ribbons, beginning at the hipline, is draped around the dress, ending in a large double bow with trailing fringed and jet-embroidered streamers at the join of the back panel and train. The only jewels are a pair of jet earrings, but here and there on the dress is the discreet glimmer of jet and iridescent beads.

It is inconceivable that any woman would have trailed down the streets in a dress such as this. Yet there were some who did, for Mrs. Oliphant, that guardian of the social flame, was evidently alluding to certain members of her gender, those whom a respectable lady of her class would choose to ignore—or of whose existence she would blissfully be unaware.

Plate 14

Dinner Gown circa 1880

During the latter part of the 1870s and early 1880s, fashion decreed that ladies adopt a look of pencil slimness. The long tapering lines of the princess cut (an extension of the cuirass bodice) produced the desired effect—providing one had the figure to carry it off!

Fortunately my Ladies possess an ideal form, as did those in the inspiring period fashion plates. However, the reality is that fashion plates and human flesh are often at odds, and pencil slimness must have been a trial for those ladies with an excess of *embonpoint* for, unlike previous fashions, the princess silhouette left no place to hide the results of too many tea cakes and bonbons.

The design of this costume is that of a redingote-like overdress pulled back to reveal an elaborate under-dress. The front section of the overdress consists of long panels of royal-purple silk satin opening into deep folds that sweep around the torso, terminating at a point in the center back just below the knees, beneath a cascade of bows with fringed tails. A separate section emerges from under the bows, spreading out into a mermaid-like train. This train is finished with a bias band of satin and a ruffle of mauve silk taffeta, and jet-beaded black lace, along with a few strategically placed bows. The back of the dress is composed of six princess-cut gores. The sleeves are elbow-length, banded in mauve silk and beaded black lace, mauve silk bows and a short flared cuff of beaded lace and silk tulle.

The under-dress section is of mauve silk taffeta, diagonally overlaid with panels of black lace embroidered with jet and iridescent beads. Between each of the lace panels is a fold of mauve silk. The hem is finished with a ruffle of mauve silk taffeta and a band of beaded lace. The neckline is square, edged with a ruche of pleated silk tulle, and accented with a bow of mauve silk.

Jet jewelry was very fashionable during the latter part of the nineteenth century, so in addition to the overall sparkle of jet on the costume, I have provided my Lady with a suite of jet jewelry, including a choker, bracelet, earrings and a tiara.

The fan that accompanies this Dinner Gown is one of two (the other is shown in Plate 11) my wife and I found in the Paris flea market. It is of tortoise with gold inlay, and a hand-painted scene on parchment. After returning home, I discovered a signature on it—Duvelroy, who was one of the better-known fan makers of nineteenth-century Paris. I don't think that we paid more than one hundred dollars for the pair. Into each life there occasionally comes a great buy!

Despite the confining fit and difficult mobility of this Dinner Gown, a lady would indulge herself at a lavish dinner of many courses, and then, afterwards, attend a grand ball. They were considered the weaker sex—but I wonder?

"At the present moment women go about hobbled after the fashion adopted by our forefathers to prevent the straying of their horses and asses when turned out to grass," was the significant comment of a contemporary, implying that such a pose was gratifying to the male sex, now becoming anxious at the prospect of feminine emancipation.

English Women's Clothing in the 19th Century
C. Willett Cunnington

Plate 15

Dinner Gown circa 1883

The fashions of the 1870s and 1880s were much inspired by those of the eighteenth century, both in design and fabric choices. The nouveau society of the nineteenth century liked to cultivate an association with anything hinting of a royal connection, which in turn might embellish their newly acquired status. Their dressmakers were only too happy to creatively assist.

Although the color combination of rich black velvet and vibrant red silk satin is definitely Victorian, certain parts of this dinner costume are reminiscent of the elegant fashions of Versailles and the Petit Trianon. The flounced sleeves, V-shaped bodice and elaborate lace-covered skirt bring to mind Boucher's portraits of Madame de Pompadour. Panier-style drapery accents the hips, and panels of black velvet sweep into a train as courtly as a minuet.

The cut of the bodice is very eighteenth century with a square neckline and an inset stomacher of red satin covered in black lace glittering with jet embroidery. The sleeves are elbow-length with deep lace flounces.

From beneath a red satin bow at the center front, the bodice curves back over the hips to a deep round at the back finished with a large satin bow. The velvet portion of the bodice is edged in jet with a line of jet fringe around the hipline.

The skirt (suggestive of an eighteenth-century petticoat) is of red satin covered with a delicate tracery of black lace shimmering with jet and steel cut beads. Panier-like draperies of red satin and lace fold back into the long black velvet train and, coming from beneath the bodice at the center back is an arrangement of loops and fringed tails of black velvet and red satin. The entire velvet skirt is lined in silk taffeta and has

a *balayeuse* of finely pleated black lace. Hidden by a deep hemline of red silk satin fringe (three layers) are red shoes as elegant as those of the Duchesse de Guermantes in Marcel Proust's *A la Recherche du Temps Perdu*.

To complete the toilette a parure of jewelry has been created consisting of earrings made from tiny steel-cut buttons from which dangle clusters of ruby beads and a necklace mounted on black velvet ribbon festooned with jet steel-cut beads and rubies. Red ostrich adorns the coiffure held in place by a steel-cut tiara (fashioned carefully from an old buckle).

All this grandeur was confined to one's own dining room, for according to *Fashions in London* by Barbara Worsley-Gough "...there were no hotels in London in which ladies could dine in a public room. The alternative was to eat in the coffee-room downstairs at a long table side by side with strangers, which of course was out of the question for a Victorian Lady."

Plate 16

Visiting Costume circa 1885

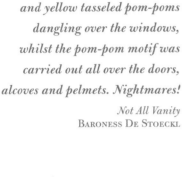

The Baroness was describing her family's 1880 Parisian drawing room which, despite her obvious distaste (in retrospect) was at the time the height of fashion. On *le jour de Maman* (her mother's reception day) this red-and-yellow extravaganza would have been "transformed into a veritable hothouse" of potted palms and huge arrangements of fragrant lilies where the ladies of the Parisian haut monde would while away the afternoon exchanging versions of the latest scandal, which was *La Vie* of 1880s Paris.

This Visiting Costume does suggest the combined skills of an upholsterer and a dress designer, and could easily blend into the red-and-yellow opulence of her mother's drawing room. The cut-away jacket is of red silk satin with a collar and cuffs of matching velvet. The closure is concealed under a satin bow at the center front, and the jacket is edged all around to the deep back point in red braid, accented with satin bows, each centered with a cluster of jet and red beads. Under the jacket is a high-necked cream-colored brocade and satin vest trimmed in ivory lace and gold buttons.

The satin underskirt has a deep pleated flounce and a wide band of red velvet and braid. The draped-up overskirt, so typical of this period, is supposed to have been inspired by the tucked-up effect created by washerwomen when plying their trade at the river's edge, and referred to in haute-couture circles as a *tablier à la blanchisseuse*, proving that high chic often has humble origins. Of course no washerwoman's skirts would have been of silk satin, nor so lavishly trimmed with such ornate braid and tasseled fringe. An 1880s-style bustle and a yellow silk taffeta petticoat support all this satin, velvet and tasseled fringe.

The high crowned hat is of red satin and velvet with a flaring inverted bow, reminiscent of the *fontange* fashion attributed to one of Louis XVI's amours—Madame La Duchesse de Fontange, of not-so-humble origins. The shoes are red satin trimmed with ivory lace, and the always-necessary parasol is done in a matching red silk taffeta with an ebony handle.

The Baroness also recalled that on "those days luncheon would be early and afterwards my Mother and Sisters used to rest, so as to be fresh for the reception. This was followed by the ordeal of dressing which meant the coiffeur, the ladies' maids and the family dressmaker who had to produce every Friday two new dresses, one for Fanita and one for Constance. My Mother also had to have a new gown designed by Worth. How times have changed since the extravagances of the eighties!"

I hope that the Baroness's critique of my Lady's Visiting Costume would have been kinder than of the efforts of her mother's decorator.

Plate 17

Reception Dress circa 1885

B y the end of the 1870s the bustle had all but vanished, but by the mid-1880s, like the fabled phoenix, it arose again in full bloom. Unlike the soft curves in fashion in the early 1870s, however, the silhouette now took on a definite projected-back appearance with draperies that assumed a heavy upholstered look.

Several years ago I acquired several panels of a rich red silk satin that had been part of a skirt. Always apprehensive about working with old fabric, I decided to have the panels dry cleaned. If they fell apart during the process then I would have saved myself many hours of labor and aggravation but, as luck would have it, they had a high survival rate, and I was ready to creatively "upholster" my Lady.

The bodice is designed in the form of an open jacket with a vest-like inset of off-white antique lace over rose silk taffeta. Three red satin bows with grosgrain tails are arranged over the lace; each bow is knotted with twists of garnet beads and clusters of glass grapes. Folds of satin extend from the standing collar to the waist area.

The satin bodice curves down to a point below the waist, then curves back over the hipline toward the back where it joins the four back-bodice gores. Each of these gores terminate in deep points which are outlined with garnet beads, as is the entire edge of the bodice. The sleeves are three-quarter length, cuffed in satin folds and bows.

For the skirt, built over a half bustle and silk petticoat, I created an underskirt of rose silk taffeta, overlaid with antique Duchesse lace and a pleated silk taffeta flounce. Over this is an asymmetrically arranged "apron" edged with garnet beading. Set into a side-back seam of the underskirt is the long red satin train, lined with a stiff cotton gauze, and finished with a *balayeuse* of pleated ivory lace. At the top of the train are clusters of satin and grosgrain ribbon dyed to match.

The Lady's hair is dressed with a diadem-like arrangement of satin and grosgrain ribbons, lightly embellished with garnet beads and glass grapes. Earrings are of garnet beads with drops of red glass. She also wears a gold locket on her corsage. Shoes are of matching red silk satin.

To keep Madame cool while performing her duties as a hostess, I have provided her with a delightful fan depicting a Spanish bull-fighting scene, which could be considered apropos of the occasion, for being a great social hostess required the dexterity of a bull fighter in order to keep one's position secure.

A lady's official Reception or At Home day to receive callers was another of those endless rituals that occupied her purposeless leisure and kept her in touch with her social equals—as well as an opportunity to display her latest delivery from the esteemed House of Worth. Although my Lady's gown is not from Worth, I have tried to create for her a toilette as luxurious and dignified as one that the great couturier might have provided.

Plate 18

Ball Gown for a Young Lady circa 1885

How reassuring for the self-esteem of the family's "ugly ducklings." Ugly or not, most young society ladies of marriageable age had to endure the debutante rituals, which swept them into a whirl of social events, wherein they could hope to catch the attention of some eligible swain—under the watchful eye of their determined mother.

For this Ball Gown I decided on a youthful color scheme of pale-pink and cream. Perhaps I was remembering the lyrics of an Irving Berlin ballad from *Annie Get Your Gun:* "The girl that I marry will have to be as soft and as pink as a nursery." (And certainly not ugly).

The multiple-gored bodice of pink silk *gros de londres* is cut in the typical style of the period, pointed front and back. Fine cream-colored lace is draped in a wrap-around fashion, meeting at one side under a pink bow. Similar bows are placed on each shoulder, and a delicate garland of ribbon trim is applied at the neckline and around the edge of the bodice.

The upper part of the skirt is composed of a polonaise drape in the front, with bouffant back drapery, both of pink *gros de londres* edged in lace and the garland ribbon trim. The back drapery is drawn into a large bow with fringed ends. A simi-

lar, but smaller, bow finishes the deep point of the back bodice. Both bows are embellished with knots of crystal beads and glass flowers.

The underskirt is of cream-colored silk taffeta with an overskirt of fine cotton net to which are attached alternating rows of pleated silk tulle and delicate cream-colored lace. At the very hem is a row of pleated silk taffeta.

As young ladies were not supposed to appear in a lavish display of jewels (that would hopefully come later), I felt that a simple pair of freshwater pearls and crystal earrings would be appropriate. A pink ribbon around the neck, a pink lace fan and pink flowers in the hair complete the toilette of this fashionable young Lady. Her dancing shoes are of pink *gros de londres*, bowed in pink satin ribbon.

This "habiliment" of pink and cream should assure even the less favored—unless she be completely devoid of social graces—a swarm of eligible swains, and the inspiring prospect of wedding bells.

Plate 19

Wedding Gown circa 1885

By the mid-1880s the bustle was enjoying its swan song, though it was not to vanish meekly. This was the period of the enormous back projection or *tournure* (remember, the term "bustle" was considered a bit common and these alternatives had a much more elegant ring).

For this Wedding Gown I combined a superb piece of nineteenth-century silk satin with an exquisite piece of lace that had once adorned a blouse bearing a Worth label.

The lace pattern was composed of two beautiful baskets of flowers, along with a delicate border. I decided to use the floral baskets as focal points, one on the front skirt, and the other near the end of the long train.

I was able to cut the skirt front from a single piece of the lace, but the arrangement on the train required a careful cutting-out of the basket motif and border, and then appliquéing them to the satin. I then proceeded to highlight the pattern with pearl and crystal embroidery—a time-consuming but gratifying project.

The satin bodice is cut with a pointed front and back, fastening up the center front. This closure is completely hidden by an elaborate plastron of satin and beaded lace, framed with a satin border from which hangs a deep fringe of crystal beads. The plastron is sewn to one side of the bodice and caught to the other by a series of hooks and thread loops.

The lace portion of the skirt ends where the train begins. The train is completely separate, attached to the skirt by a series of concealed hooks. It is made of silk satin, lined with silk taffeta and interlined with a thin layer of cotton wadding, which produces a very lush effect.

The most dramatic details of this Wedding Gown are lavished on the back projection. At the very top is a large lace-appliquéd satin bow, the ends fringed in long strands of pearl and crystal. Caught up into the bow are folds of satin festooned with more of the crystal and pearl fringe, and clusters of "wax" orange blossoms. To achieve the effect of wax flowers I used tiny gauze lilacs, which I coated with several layers of an acrylic gloss varnish.

Accessories include a lace fan (an occasional substitute for a bouquet), pearl earrings and a wreath of "wax" orange blossoms, to which is attached a long veil of silk illusions.

The raison d'etre for the creation of Les Petites Dames de Mode was my desire to expand my creative horizon and to serve as an escape from the bridal world that was my real-life career. My creative horizon did expand but, I soon realized, despite my momentary attack of boredom with white and ivory, that an escape from wedding gowns was not to be. After all, the wedding gown is without doubt the most romantic expression of feminine attire; how could I abandon it? Besides, it had been my long interest in period costume that had provided me with much source material during my designing years and, as a result, I found it quite easy to move from the contemporary bridal world into one in which I recreate the fashions of another time.

So—here's to wedding gowns, they are obviously part of my heritage!

Plate 20

The Elegant Widow circa 1886

Black was primarily reserved for elderly ladies and mourning, but judging from the amount of black dresses in every collection, one might assume that grieving was a full-time occupation. Victorian etiquette for observing death was strict, complicated and far-reaching, owing to an endless supply of relatives.

I felt that a mourning costume should be represented in my collection of Petites Dames. Though such costumes were supposed to be as drab as possible, sorrow is so much easier to endure if one is attired with a certain chic.

The complicated design of this mourning costume is developed in a combination of velvet, brocade, lace, silk fringe and silk faille, with a great deal of jet embroidery. The close-fitting bodice of silk faille is cut in several gores, flaring out over the hips and bustle, lavishly trimmed with jet and silk fringe. The front opens to display a faux vest of black silk brocade, the opening defined by a narrow panel of velvet edged in lace. The long sleeves are cuffed in black velvet with jet trim.

An apron-like overskirt of silk brocade is asymmetrically draped around the upper portion of the skirt. (This silk brocade was originally a pair of sleeves with just enough material for me to work with). The underskirt is made up from a piece of silk faille, discovered in one of my flea-market forays, with the beautiful braid and jet embroidery still intact. With careful manipulation I was able to shape the skirt without removing the embroidery (a stressful prospect at best). An opening on the left

side reveals an inset of pleating. Silk and grosgrain-ribbon fringe cascades down both sides of the opening and encircles the entire hemline.

The bonnet accompanying this toilette is of black velvet and silk faille, trimmed in jet and ostrich feathers, with a long floating veil of silk chiffon to add a graceful touch of melancholy. There is also a muff of black velvet, bowed in brocade and literally dripping in jet. Protruding from the muff is a white handkerchief bordered in black, should a moment of grief overcome the Lady.

A charming accessory is a tiny gold locket suspended from a satin bow over the Lady's heart. This is one of those wonderful antique-shop finds, and made to order for this costume, for when the locket is opened the face of a very handsome gentleman appears, surrounded by a lock of hair. Could this be for whom she mourns?

Wealthy, chic and beautiful, my Elegant Widow, methinks, will not stay a widow for long.

Plate 21

Promenade and Visiting Toilette circa 1886

On exhibition my Elegant Widow, standing by her departed's tombstone, surrounded by her sisters in their colorful and opulent toilettes, always seems isolated and sad. By the strict etiquette of Victorian mourning, a widow found herself virtually ostracized socially, and confined to what must have seemed a perpetual state of gloom. So I decided she should have a friend to brighten up her solitude. Of course, her friend's gown should be reasonably conservative, considering the setting, but no less stylish.

The fashions of the latter 1880s, because of the very pronounced back projection and the emphasis on upholstery-like fabrics, elaborate beading, heavy fringes and braids, took on an imposing and majestic appearance. While wandering around in a vintage-clothing store, I came upon a shoulder cape, which was devoid of all its trim. It was of voided velvet consisting of a small black velvet floral pattern against a soft-brown background. When I combined this with a piece of iridescent brown/blue silk taffeta, from my ever-present scrap inventory, I felt that I had the correct elegant but conservative combination suitable for a visit of consolation among the tombstones.

The velvet bodice is cut in the tight-fitting 1880s style, pointed in front with a deep, rounded back. A slim pointed plastron of the silk taffeta, bordered with a narrow band of jet embroidered lace, conceals the front opening. The bodice hem is finished with a delicate corded braid, as are the sleeves.

Brown silk taffeta, in the panier style, swathes the hips, meeting with two large bouffant taffeta drapes crushed into a bow at the center back. These draperies fall in deep points, outlined with the lace and jet trim, and fringed in jet drops.

The underskirt is cut entirely from the voided velvet with a hem of the corded braid. A narrow box pleating of the silk taffeta finishes the skirt. A small crino-

line based on one advertised in the 1885 *Harper's Bazar* called the Panier Skirt supports the skirt and a lace-trimmed cotton petticoat.

The hat with its tall crown is of the same velvet, edged with braid, with a silk taffeta bow consisting of five different length loops, secured with a jet ornament. A rakish brown ostrich feather completes this millinery confection.

A faux watch is pinned just above the bosom (she has other appointments and punctuality is the sign of a lady). Her earrings are made from a pair of enamel buttons and, of course, there is the ever-present parasol of black silk and lace and a bow of silk taffeta.

I'm sure the Widow is pleased to have the company of a friend, and I would not be surprised if the conversation, after a few words of sympathy, might turn to the subject of fashion. Perhaps it is time to move on to the more attractive shades of mauve and lilac permitted for the final stage of mourning—a trip to the dressmaker would be so uplifting!

Plate 22

Toilette de Bal circa 1888

The Baroness's recollections of her life in the luxurious atmosphere of the haut monde are interesting indeed. All that resting in order to look fresh, but then a lady in the position of the Baroness could never resort to make-up (they referred to it as "paint").

Only those Jezebels of the shady demimonde could "tart" themselves up with paint. Respectable ladies might discreetly apply a bit of powder to the nose, if it glowed unbecomingly, but other than that a perpetual state of resting appears to have been their only recourse to improving nature.

Fortunately, my Ladies enjoy a state of permanent freshness requiring no resting whatsoever. Their only concern is looking good, and that can at times take a definite toll on *my* freshness!

The account of the Baroness concerning her preparations for an evening out inspired me to create a Toilette de Bal that I hoped would justify those endless hours of resting. Searching through my inventory I found a rectangular silk lace scarf in a pale shade of gold and a length of silk that matched perfectly. With the addition of pearls and crystal, I decided that I could provide a gown splendid enough for a thoroughly rested and fresh-looking Baroness.

Twelve gores make up the sleekly fitting silk bodice; the shoulders are discreetly veiled in poufs of lace and swags of pearls. Folds of the lace are draped over the low, V-shaped neckline with more swags of pearls caught into a cluster of crystal drops. A large crushed bow of silk and lace adorns the back of the bodice.

The front of the foundation skirt is of the gold silk, overlaid with soft folds of lace held in place by a scattering of iridescent pearls. The hem is of silk fringe over a short flounce of pleated lace.

The *tournure* supports a long train of the pale-gold silk over which falls an elaborate cascade of lace shimmering with iridescent crystal drops and pearls. (The center section of the rectangular lace scarf was used for the front of the skirt and the remaining end pieces for the train).

Such an elegant Toilette required something special in the way of jewels. Earrings and necklace are of a combination of pearls, peridot, amethyst and citrine, and for the headpiece a diadem of twisted pearls and crystal drops. The fan is of swansdown.

And—would it all be worth it? In the words of the Baroness: "...and so we would all go on to another party, perhaps a ball. A struggle to go up the stairs, crowds trying to do the same; endeavoring to dance holding those long trains; at last home! And being persuaded that it had been a wonderful evening. Looking back one may say how could one enjoy life then? And yet one did, immensely: it was all so grand."

Chapter 5

La Fin de Siècle
The 1890s

In the last decade of the nineteenth century, fashion devised a new shape for the ladies to adapt to: the hourglass figure. The ideal was to achieve the smallest waist measurement possible, which gave rise to that legendary eighteen-inch waist associated with everyone's grandmother. Judging from the surviving garments of the period it was more a rarity than a reality. Very tight corseting notwithstanding, the design of 1890s dresses could easily contribute to rumors of exaggerated waistline circumferences. Actually, it was an optical illusion created by the combination of the massive, shoulder-widening leg-of-mutton sleeves; the cleverly contrived V-shaped bodice detailing, which drew the eye to the center of the waistline; and the sweeping, multi-gored skirt fanning outward to the hemline. In the hands of a skillful dressmaker, such a calculated arrangement of design could provide even a lady of excessive amplitude with a fashionable appearance.

This was the Gilded Age, and flaunting one's wealth was not considered bad taste, but almost an obligation. Was not the rise from rags to riches part of the American dream, and displaying it an inspiration to others? Every delicious and extravagant detail was dutifully reported in the society columns, and who wore what where was eagerly absorbed by the masses. A lady's social activities, be she attending the opera or performing her proscribed works of charity, demanded an endless array of elegant toilettes fashioned from sumptuous silks, velvets and brocades, embellished with lace, furs, intricate beading and embroideries. Elaborately constructed and fortified with stiff linings and inter-linings to keep the entire effect in place, the ladies appeared to be encased in yards of fabric armor.

Everything about the Gilded Age could be described as grand, splendid, magnificent or opulent. Money was no object, even if it was acquired from coal mines, steel mines or railroads. It bought marble mansions, gowns by Worth and European titles for daughters whose grandparents had not so long ago trekked across the wilderness in covered wagons, dodging tomahawks and rattlesnakes.

By the late 1890s the opulent stiff fabrics and huge sleeves began to succumb to the inevitable progress of fashion. A softer silhouette would soon appear. There was also a feverish excitement in the air at the approach of a new century, with anticipation of great things to come. A wonderful and modern world was predicted, and it would be known as La Belle Epoque.

Plate 23

Wedding Gown circa 1893

*At the age of eighteen each girl
put up her hair; a visible
signal that says, unmistakably,
that a woman is open to offers.*

The Edwardian Lady
KATE CAFFREY

Offers of marriage, that is! In a flurry of activity, the young innocent was often snatched from the schoolroom and thrust into her first "season" (actually the marriage market), at the end of which, it was to be hoped, an engagement would be announced. After a proper lapse of time, she would move in a slow and timorous progress down a church aisle, resplendent in a wedding gown, while her mama, the chief organizer of this rite of passage, would sigh in relief, having saved a daughter from a fate worse than death—spinsterhood!

This Wedding Gown was inspired by an interesting drawing I came across in the May 1893 issue of *The Delineator* magazine. It showed a princess-style dress in which the entire front was cut in one piece of goods, from neck to hem, with five darts controlling the fit. The designer/engineer in me could not resist the challenge!

After a trial run in muslin, I decided upon a piece of cream-colored, pure silk *gros de londres* for the final endeavor, because of its wonderful molding quality. Combined with a silk lining (plus an interlining of cotton organdy half way up from the hem) the five-dart construction worked like a charm. The back consists of six princess panels flowing into a long sweeping train.

Fashion writers of the period cautioned that simplicity in wedding attire was to be desired, and more in keeping with the solemnity of the occasion. Actually, the beautiful richness of the fabric dictated only a minimum of decoration, so I decided to use a self-fabric twisted braid trimming, often seen on gowns of the period. It completely edges the hem, with a bow at each seam, and also trims the sleeves and upper bodice.

Huge leg-of-mutton sleeves were the dernier cri of the 1890s, ballooning about the upper arm, but tightly fitted from the elbow to wrist (trying to maneuver all that fullness into the armhole of a 29-inch figure can really be quite stressful!)

Simplicity has its place. A wedding gown, however, demands at least a touch of lace. A flounce of this delicate fabric floats over the gathered cap of the sleeves and fills in the upper area of the bodice and the lower arm of the sleeves.

The long silk tulle veil is secured to a high headdress of wired pearls that would have trembled slightly, creating an aura of modesty that the bride was expected to display as she made her way down the aisle to join her intended.

Grand-society marriages were often determined by social aspirations, or family or financial considerations—sometimes by all three. Like lambs led to the slaughter, the bride went down the aisle dressed in splendor, but generally without a clue as to her wifely "duties" (other than seeing that the servants behaved and dressing well). Somehow or other, after having said "I do," a young girl was automatically transformed into a woman of the world. The realization that babies were not delivered down the chimney by storks or found under rose bushes must have been quite unnerving.

Plate 24

Grande Robe de Bal circa 1893

Thomas Edison's contribution to the world—and its ballrooms—of the electric light seems to have been responsible for this "yellow" trend by embellishing it with an added golden glow. Not only were vivid colors part of the 1890s fashion scene, but it was popular to emphasize the huge sleeves by having them cut in a different color from the rest of the dress.

Yellow happens to be a color I rather fancy (probably because I'm a Leo), and during a sojourn to one of my fabric haunts I came across this yellow silk satin, brocaded with sprays of cherry blossoms in shades of cream, deep ivory and dark brown. To achieve the fashionable mix, I was able to find a matching brown silk taffeta for the sleeves—and my "golden" lady was on her way!

The bodice is in the pointed front and back style, with a square neckline dropping to a V in back. The neckline is framed with a band of coffee-colored lace, and a stomacher of crystal, pearl and yellow-beaded flowers extends the front neckline treatment into a deep V. Bows of brown silk with beaded centers and cream and brown silk tassels accent the square design of the neckline. A row of pearls, crystal and yellow beads edges the bodice.

The skirt is cut in the full sweeping style of the 1890s with a long train. The hem is finished with satin cording, a hint of dark-brown lace, and a *balayeuse* of pleated ivory lace.

Underneath is a full-trained petticoat of cream silk taffeta with a deep pleated flounce. The rustle of silk taffeta gave off a sound that was considered a bit seductive. (Those Victorians were not all prim and proper).

To further embellish an already beautiful fabric I decided, rather than "gilding the lily," to gild the cherry blossoms by hand-beading all the sprays with clusters of pearls, crystal and yellow beads. Might as well take full advantage of Mr. Edison's wonderful invention!

Such splendor requires the extra sparkle of jewels. Attached to a brown silk ribbon are rows of yellow "diamonds," pearls and crystal drops. The earrings are composed of gold beads and crystal drops. Madame's tiara, styled to fit her authentic coiffure, is made of gilded metal from sections of an old bracelet, interspersed with rows of yellow "diamonds." A large ostrich-feather fan completes the ensemble, making this a dress that does indeed reflect all the glitter and gold of that opulent moment in time now known as The Gilded Age.

Plate 25

Columbian Exposition Evening Gown circa 1893

The liveliest fancy could scarcely conjure up a vision of magnificence equal to that which entrances the visitor to the great World's Fair.
THE DELINEATOR, MAY 1893

Since the 1871 incident with Mrs. O'Leary's rambunctious cow, Chicago (still considered a social backwater by the eastern "aristocracy") had arisen from the ashes and was ready to welcome one and all (even easterners) to the greatest event of the century. The Columbian Exposition, the four-hundredth anniversary celebration of the discovery of America by Columbus created a whirl of grand functions among Chicago's social elite, and the ladies required equally grand toilettes for these events.

My Columbian Exposition Evening Gown was inspired by the discovery of an unusual length of black lace (nine inches wide by ten yards long) in a dealer's booth at a large doll event. The pattern was of Spanish galleons floating on a lacy sea with a scalloped border of anchors. This was something rare that I knew I would never see again and, bearing in mind that "he who hesitates is lost"—I bought it! All ten yards for one hundred dollars—nothing is too good for my Ladies.

The question then was to which period did it belong? I flipped open my little black book and rang up my friend Doris May, an internationally respected guru on lace. We talked; I faxed; she thought and, being on her way to Paris the following week, decided to make some inquires in the City of Light. It worked—mystery solved! The particular pattern was woven in 1892 in Calais, France, and was called the *Carvel de Columbus*. Now I had not only the correct period but a wonderful event with which to associate the lace.

I decided to use a pale-pink silk taffeta for the basic dress combined with a slightly deeper shade of silk satin for the sleeves, bows and bias fold that encircles the skirt. The main attraction is, of course, the deep flounce with its flotilla of ships eased on across the skirt front, and gathering fullness as it moves around the long spreading train. There is also an under-flounce of silk tulle, just enough to give support to the lace. The scale of the lace pattern is just right for the size of the mannequins, one of those happy happenings.

To cover the joining of the lace to the skirt I used a bias fold of silk satin, with an inset of narrow jet-beaded lace. Satin bows, with jet centers, are placed at intervals along the bias fold.

The bodice is tightly fitted with a low curving neckline outlined with narrow jet-beaded lace, and garlanded with a ring of satin bows. From beneath the bows is suspended a glittering jet fringe. A row of the narrow jet-beaded lace finishes the bottom of the bodice.

For accessories I provided a simple velvet ribbon around the neck, jet earrings and a jet tiara, pink silk shoes and a fan of peacock feathers. Surely this lady would have caused quite a stir at one of the evening receptions given by Mrs. Palmer Potter, one of the mover and shakers of the Exposition, and Chicago's answer to New York's Mrs. William Backhouse Astor, Jr. (the Backhouse was eliminated for obvious reasons), the undisputed queen of society's four hundred.

Plate 26

Wedding Gown circa 1894

Brides were advised to camouflage their newlywed status on their honeymoons. In William Dean Howells' Their Wedding Journey, Isabel, a twenty-seven-year-old bride, nervously asked her husband: "We shall not strike the public as bridal, shall we? My one horror in life is an evident bride."

The Light of the Home—
An Intimate View of the Lives of
Women in Victorian America
HARVEY GREEN

The hourglass look is quite apparent in the styling of this 1890s Wedding Gown, which would have been deemed most suitable for a quiet wedding in the front parlor. The exaggerated leg-of-mutton sleeves broaden the shoulderline while the delicate lace plastron, concealing the front opening, draws the eye to the center of the waist like a V, which then reverses itself as the skirt spreads out toward the wide hemline. Tight corseting notwithstanding, the legendary "wasp waist" was not so much nature's work as a simple triangular balancing act.

The plastron is made from a two-inch-wide piece of fine border lace, framed in twisted satin ribbon, and a softly gathered lace ruching. The lace is lightly embroidered with seed pearls that also form knots on the satin-ribbon bows.

The cream silk brocade is from an actual wedding gown worn in 1894 and given to me by the bride's daughter. It had seen several members of the family to the altar, undergoing quite drastic alterations in the process. Any resemblance to the original dress was completely lost and the silk was suffering from several breaks, but considering that the lady had taken the trouble to send it to me, I felt obliged to be creative. I made up a couple of muslin models and, after perfecting the pattern pieces, laid them out on the brocade, carefully avoiding the damaged areas. Some of the panels required piecing (which was a common practice in full-scale gowns of the period) and a complete lining of silk organdy provided relief for any strain on the brocade. As I mentioned before, using old fabric can be treacherous but with care, determination, crossed fingers, a "sip" or two of scotch, things can have a happy conclusion. Did I forget to mention "luck?"

The bridal veil is made of two panels of very fine lace originally intended as a lady's neckpiece. It is worked in a series of loops on a satin ribbon in a sort of coronet style, with wide trailing ends.

Large elaborate society weddings took place with much fanfare to the delight of the public, who were consumed with curiosity about the doings of their "betters." That curiosity was satisfied in the social columns the next day. (Consuelo Vanderbilt was appalled at the erroneous and detailed reports of her trousseau—but after all, the groom was an authentic English duke!)

In spite of the curiosity factor, however, such spectacular weddings were not felt to be quite in keeping with the delicacy of the bridal image. Exchanging vows beneath a virginal bower of roses in one's own drawing-room, surrounded by one's family, was closer to the Victorian ideal of propriety. In fact the etiquette books cautioned bridal couples when on their "wedding journey" (honeymoon) to call as little attention as possible to their newly married status. I think the rules have since changed.

Plate 27

Ball Gown circa 1894

light gathered puffs at the end of the 1880s, sleeves exploded by the mid-1890s into vast balloon shapes that presented as many problems to the ladies as had the vast hoop skirts of the 1860s. Not only did these sleeves require large amounts of fabric, but they involved a great deal of construction and support, and one's dancing partner had to stay at arm's length.

This particular rich shade of reddish-purple silk satin used for this Ball Gown is a donation from my wife's evening wardrobe. It represents the leftover material from a ball gown, with matching coat, that I created for her in 1986 when we (who are waltz addicts) journeyed to Vienna to attend the legendary Opera Ball. In true Viennese style we danced until dawn—a little hard on the feet, but great for the spirit!

To embellish the satin I found a piece of black silk lace in an interesting pattern of deep scallops. This lace covers the bodice, which has an open square neckline graduating into a deep V in the back. The front of the bodice is heavily appliquéd with black velvet flowers and embroidered with a mixture of amethyst beads and jet. A thick roping of this embroidery is applied over the shoulders to the center back. The full sleeves are gathered in the center and covered with an all-over scattering of beads.

The skirt is cut in nine flaring gores. A deep row of the scalloped lace is applied to the lower part of the skirt, and liberally adorned with the amethyst beading. Another row of beading finishes the hemline. Two petticoats support the skirt: one is floor length of white silk taffeta, and the other is a black silk taffeta with a train, flounced in pleated *point d'esprit*.

Around the Lady's neck is a black velvet ribbon, "dripping" with jet. Her earrings are also jet, as is the tiara. An added touch of elegance is a trailing stole of the finest silk tulle appliquéd with delicate lace medallions—completely impractical but so effective.

In the world of high style the preservation of a lady's sleeves took precedence over all else, for comfort and convenience were not requisites for fashion in those far-away days. The *elegantes* of society were not particularly concerned about these "minor" inconveniences, which might be termed a form of graceful bondage. What the husbands thought is not known.

Plate 28

Watering Place Toilette circa 1895

In fashionable places very fashionable attire is necessary.

Etiquette for Women: A Book of
Modern Modes and Manners
BY ONE OF THE ARISTOCRACY

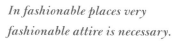

Inhabitants of the beau monde retreated periodically to various watering places and spas to recoup from their exhausting round of social duties, and to rest for the next round. However, there were still rules and rituals to be observed. Morning and afternoon strolls to sip restorative mineral waters required suitable costumes for the promenade of fashion. Ladies would arrive at these grand hotels with great steamer trunks filled with ravishing toilettes, certain to bring the rocking chairs on the hotel verandas to a screeching halt.

For my "invalid's" medicinal promenade I chose a beautiful crisp silk taffeta of aqua and cream stripes, and a soft-rose faille. The stripes are arranged diagonally on the bodice. Over the front closure, starting at the collar, a shaped plastron of rose faille extends down the bodice to the waist, where it becomes part of a wide girdle-like belt that circles the waistline, terminating in a bow at the center back.

The sleeves are extremely full with a lining of silk organdy in the puffed section. There is also a fitted under-sleeve of silk taffeta to which the puffed section is sewn, controlling the fullness. From the elbow area down, the under-sleeve is covered with the striped material, and has a cuff of rose faille and Irish lace. The bolero jacket is of pieces of Irish lace appliquéd to a cotton net foundation.

Thirteen gores, each one lined in white silk taffeta, make up the skirt. The problem of matching stripes can bring on a migraine, especially when you have limited fabric. On the center of each of the thirteen gore-pattern pieces (which were all alike in size), I marked a stripe line, which I lined up on the fabric. As a result, when the panels were joined, all the stripes fell into the correct position—and I was Advil-free!

The hat is in the boater style, in white silk taffeta covered with Irish lace. The hatband is of the striped taffeta with a cluster of bow-loops in the striped taffeta and rose faille.

A parasol of rose faille and a deep lace ruffle protects the Lady's delicate complexion, and caught at her waist is a charming steel purse for her "mad money"—another antique-shop find. I trust that this lovely costume would have lifted the spirits of the "invalid," for as Mrs. Eric Pritchard wrote in her book, *The Cult of Chiffon*: "Nothing is so conducive to 'sangfroid' (composure) as an innate feeling that one is well dressed."

Plate 29

Evening Gown circa 1896

Old New York society was constantly vigilant against flashy rich new people who were always trying to cross the social barriers. Allowing one's new French dresses to "mellow" for a year (Boston was more conservative) was a way to distinguish the established from the upstarts.

The House of Worth was noted not only for its splendid dresses, but also for the magnificent and unique textile designs from which these garments were made. Certain motifs were associated with the firm, especially larger-than-life florals (roses, irises and hydrangeas), as well as certain insects such as dragonflies and butterflies.

There is an interesting Worth gown of ice-blue satin woven with butterflies shown in the book *The Opulent Years* by Elizabeth Ann Coleman. Several years ago someone gave me a short length of cream-colored silk organdy woven with black butterflies. Needless to say, I knew exactly what I was going to do with it—move over, Mr. Worth!

The skirt was the first challenge. The butterflies were placed very symmetrically on the organdy and I wanted them to "fly" randomly over the skirt. I carefully placed each of the skirt-pattern pieces on the organdy with the butterflies spaced a little differently on each section. From the fall-out scraps I removed the butterflies and appliquéd them wherever I wanted them to fly. I then lightly embroidered the entire skirt and butterflies with tiny silver sequins (like having both butterflies and fireflies). The delicate shade of pink is created by layering the cream-colored silk organdy over ivory silk taffeta lined with pink organdy.

The sleeves and bodice are cut from the same combination of fabrics. The neckline is worked with antique black lace, pink silk satin and groupings of velvet flowers. A sash of satin and black velvet ribbon crosses the bodice from shoulder to waist, wrapping itself around the body and ending in a cluster of flowers and a bow at one side.

The necklace, bracelet and tiara are of pink pearls; the earrings are made from tiny enamel buttons with pink roses. The fan is pink lace and the shoes are of pink satin with an appliquéd butterfly on each one.

Of course, Miss Jackson's commentary was in reference to the days of her youth in the 1870s. By the 1890s, although the intrepid social climbers were still kept at a distance, it was no longer considered vulgar to be fashionable (save perhaps in Boston).

"In my youth," Miss Jackson rejoined, "it was considered vulgar to dress in the newest fashions; and Amy Sillerton has always told me that in Boston the rule was to put away one's Paris dresses for two years."

The Age of Innocence
EDITH WHARTON

Plate 30

Paris Autumn Toilette circa 1896

Fashion periodicals of the day were filled with references to past centuries when describing late-nineteenth-century costumes. The wide *revers* of this silk ottoman costume and the cream silk vest and lace cravat would have been regarded as of eighteenth-century inspiration. Hints of masculinity are also evident, for pilfering of bits and pieces of men's wear was becoming common, and must have made the ladies feel rather assertive, though such items were usually given a feminine interpretation.

The ottoman silk was an earlier gift (unused and still on the roll) from the same lady who had presented me with the remains of her mother's 1894 wedding gown (Plate 25). The ottoman had been acquired for the bride's mother-in-law-to-be, but never used, allegedly because the bride did not care for it. (I trust her opinion was tactfully expressed).

To reflect the popular tailor-made image, and following the words of *Harper's Bazar*, I designed a cut-away jacket, which is hooked in place to the vest. The revers,

standing collar and cuffs are velvet, trimmed with a narrow guipure lace embroidered with lavender and garnet beads. The cuffs have deep lace ruffles, another eighteenth-century affectation. The front of the vest is covered in finely pleated chiffon and guipure lace. A delicate ornament of gold, pearl and diamond is suspended from a lace jabot at the neckline.

The umbrella-style skirt is composed of eleven gores with the characteristic 1890s flare at the hem. It is lined in a stiff white silk taffeta and the hemline is bound in velvet and trimmed with beaded guipure lace. A silk taffeta petticoat gives support and creates that lovely rustle when the Lady moves.

The hat is covered in the ottoman silk and trimmed in dark-red satin. The fashion of the period favored small hats with strange little outcroppings shooting upwards to emphasize height. Her boots are dark-red satin, as is the parasol.

Madame surveys her fashionable world through a lorgnette of tortoise-shell and silver, an accessory preferred more for the elegant chic of its effect than as a visual aid.

Plate 31

French Promenade Toilette circa 1896

While husbands made the family fortunes, their wives created the social scene in which to display it. From their marble mansions they stood guard over the endless rituals that governed their days from morning to night, along with the rules that must be adhered to if one were to be part of this exclusive society. All this activity required an enormous wardrobe, and the ultimate source could only be found in Paris at the House of Worth, where one could be confident of the perfect toilette for every occasion.

For a Promenade Toilette of "undisputed opulence," I decided to use a moiré silk in lovely shades of mauve, combined with an accent of deep-purple silk taffeta. Much attention at this time was concentrated on the upper bodice which, in addition to the huge sleeves, contributed to the illusion of the hourglass waist. In keeping with this concept I arranged a series of silk taffeta folds over the bosom (sometimes referred to as a "pouter-pigeon" look), framed in self-fabric trim and pleated lace. The high neckband (standard for daywear) supports a pleated lace ruff (Elizabethan influence?).

Between the sleeves, tightly fitted bodice and constricting collar, the lady's upright posture was undeniably assured. Three purple silk bows with centers of purple beads

and glass grapes adorn the front bodice, and a wide belt of the purple silk draws the eye to the slim waist.

The front panel of the nine-gore skirt is outlined with the self-fabric trim wound about with deep-purple silk, which ends at the hemline with a bow. This was the era of the tall woman, and designers were very inventive in ways to emphasize height—especially if one were not so blessed. The self-fabric trim and pleating continue around the hem.

Confection is the best adjective to use in describing the Lady's hat in its combination of purple and white silk taffeta, white lace and profuse application of lilacs. The indispensable parasol is of white silk taffeta with a scattering of purple bows and a handle of antique ivory. In the fashionable society of the fin de siècle, having accumulated all that wealth, it would have been considered hardly worth the effort if it were not properly displayed—and the ladies and Worth were more than willing to collaborate in that effort.

Plate 52

Evening Toilette circa 1895

*The crucial question in New York
was whether or not Mrs. Astor knew
you...Most important had she
invited you to her annual ball?
If not, you'd best leave town or
sit at home in the dark lest
anyone know your shame.*

To Marry an English Lord
CAROL MCD.WALLACE & GAIL MCCOLL

A ball during the gilded age at one of the great marble "cottages" at Newport or in Mrs. Astor's New York ballroom, which would only accommodate four hundred of the select, must have been a dazzling affair. The majority of the ladies would have been gowned by Worth (anything less would have constituted a fashion faux pas), and one can only imagine the scene: the gorgeous dresses, the jewels, the gilded ballroom and glittering chandeliers, the scent of roses, lilies and orchids and a full orchestra playing Strauss. All this and taxes had not yet been invented!

Competing with a Worth gown is not an easy task, but I thought I would give it a try. Hopefully the master will not haunt me!

Pale-aquamarine silk seemed a suitable choice with a lavish application of beaded embroidery. No time for restraint. The balloon sleeves literally drip with gold, crystal and pearl beadwork. Cream-colored chiffon drapes the upper neckline while the center panel of the lower bodice, profusely beaded with an unstinting hand, accentuates the curving lines of the figure.

The centerpiece of the nine-gore skirt is the embroidered front panel, where I nearly lost control of my "unstinting" hand. From the heavily beaded bodice, along the seam lines, descend two rows of beading—a virtual torrent of pearls, crystal and gold beading and pearl and iridescent crystal drops that engulfs clusters of crystal-covered flowers as it reaches the hemline. Swags of crystal flowers drape across the bead-studded panel that shimmers like the after-glow of fireworks. The hem of the dress is bordered with lace flowers and chiffon pleating.

If the glitter of one's dress was not enough, one could always turn to the family vault for help. A dog collar of pearls (made fashionable by Alexandra, Princess of Wales) and drop crystal earrings were fine for starters, but no lady of social standing could appear without a tiara, which conveyed an impression of devotion to things royal. Grace Vanderbilt, another formidable hostess of the gilded age, once lamented that, should a revolution reach American shores, she would be the first to go to the block like "poor dear Marie Antoinette." For my society Lady, I composed a tiara of crystal attached to her coiffeur with loops of pearls—her only fate might someday involve an auction block.

It has been said that the society lady's main occupation was her wardrobe and its acquisition. Semi-annual trips had to be made to Paris involving not only a lengthy journey, but hours debating the merits of a myriad of fabric choices, consultations with dressmakers (possibly the great Worth himself might grace her presence), and more endless hours of fittings. So dreadfully tiresome, but so very chic—and what tales to be told later in Milwaukee!

Chapter 6

La Belle Epoque 1900-1914

In 1900 the twentieth century burst on the scene accompanied by a wild euphoria. With the opening of the Universal Exhibition, Paris became the center of the cultural universe, awash with kings and queens, entrepreneurs, the rich, the famous and the infamous, Russian Grand Dukes and shady ladies of the night. The formidable Queen Victoria (who was rarely amused) died at Osborne House on the Isle of Wight in 1901. Her formal and stuffy court was taken over by the affable and portly Edward VII, with his beautiful Queen Alexandra, and the glittering and fashionable Edwardian Age was off and running. Lights blazed again at Buckingham Palace and its ballroom sparkled with diamond tiaras, as the British and American haute monde mingled in what would eventually become International Society.

Between 1900 and 1914 fashion, like Art Nouveau, decreed that the shortest distance between two points was best achieved by a curved line. Nowhere were these curves more evident than in the sweeping cut of the skirts. Multi-gored, they fit with seductive precision over rounded hips, from where they swirled out in graceful fullness, like an inverted lily, supported by rustling silk taffeta petticoats.

Toward the middle of the decade the inverted lily began to wilt. The swirling fullness became straighter as the waistline rose until, in 1910, a quasi-Empire look developed. A definite sheath-like mode was becoming evident which, in turn, between 1911 and 1913, was followed by the dubious charms of the confining hobble skirt. For some inexplicable reason, these sheath-like costumes were accessorized with hats of enormous proportion, surmounted with enough plumage to send the entire ostrich population scurrying for sanctuary.

Sir Winston Churchill remarked in his memoirs that "the old world in its sunset was fair to see." This was an apt description of La Belle Epoque, especially if one were a lady of the upper class, fashionably gowned and jeweled, drifting aimlessly through her secure and exclusive world, oblivious of what lay outside. In 1914 a pistol shot in one of those strange little Balkan countries would reverberate around the world, and that fair sunset would be no more.

Plate 33

Wedding Gown circa 1900

There are few women (and probably few men) who have not remarked the recent changes in the contour of the fashionable woman of today. The back appears to be straighter; with the bust a little lower and the abdomen less prominent; and the waistline, instead of being exactly horizontal, descends a little from the back to front.

"Fashions for September 1900"
THE DELINEATOR, 1900

The article goes on to explain that this recent change of contour is the result of the newer style of corset. It also informs its readers that the term generally applied to the new lines or contours is the "Marie Antoinette Dip." To associate the ill-fated queen of France with a change in neckwear would seem more likely than a waistline variance, but there is no accounting for the vagaries of fashion terminology.

The ideal of fashion during the Edwardian years was the tall mature woman of "splendid form," full-bosomed and well-rounded of hip. It was not a time when fashion was complimentary to the young. Their time would come in the 1920s, when the ideal was to be "flat as a board," and the "mature" woman would frantically try to flatten out those voluptuous contours that her corset had once controlled.

One of the most desirable and much-used materials of the Belle Epoque was lace, both for its beauty and because everyone knew how expensive it was (an important consideration during this opulent period). I was fortunate to have this beautiful specimen, which is sometimes referred to as Princess Lace. It was given to me by a friend who discovered it under a piece of scenery in a theater company. It was originally a skirt, but someone had cut a large section from it, probably to repair or decorate a costume. Despite that desecration there remained enough to gown my bride in luxury.

In order to preserve the design of the lace, I did not want to cut into it and, after much careful manipulation, I managed to work the piece into the skirt with only a back

seam. I would like to point out that the saw-tooth detail on the skirt is done with a narrow lace insertion. The deep flaring flounce falls from this, and is all part of the original lace skirt.

The slip lining is of silk *peau de soie* and silk organdy cut in gores matching exactly the flare of the lace skirt. All of the unmentionables are of silk including a petticoat with a deep ribbon-trimmed lace flounce.

The bodice is closed in the back and pouches in the approved manner in front, and has long full sleeves, cuffed in lace. There is an attached circular-cut bolero with cap sleeves composed of different, though harmonizing, laces. The flare of the bolero further emphasizes the pouched-look so typical of the Edwardian style. This bolero detail was designated (once again, according to *The Delineator*) as the "Monte Carlo Bolero"—no comment! The headdress consists of a "fan" of lace and silk flowers, and a long trailing veil of silk tulle, all designed to contribute to the allusion of height that the fashionable ideal now demanded.

Plate 34

Garden Party Dress circa 1900

But how lovely it must have been inside the garden for an Edwardian lady dressed to the "nines," strolling beneath the trees and among the flowers, chatting with friends, safe and secure in her perfect world. For Madame's "golden afternoon" I have confected a frock of cream-colored silk organdy over a layer of lilac silk organdy. Beneath this is a slip of lilac silk taffeta and a cream silk petticoat edged with pleated lace.

The bodice is cut with the typical dip waist and accented by a shaped lilac silk belt. A lace yoke is outlined with a bertha of pointed lace, which also forms flounces at the end of the elbow-length sleeves.

The skirt is cut in nine gores fitted at the waist and over the hips, then flares out like an inverted lily to the hem and finally trails off into a slight train. This is the standard shape of skirts from 1900 until 1902–03. Each of the seams is concealed beneath a strip of Valenciennes lace. Three rows of delicate lace encircle the hemline, shaped to conform to the flare of the skirt. Bows of lilac organdy and embroidered silk ribbon appear on the bottom of the skirt, on the sleeves and at the back closing.

Hats of La Belle Epoque were legendary: monumental in size and overloaded with flowers, feathers, ribbons and stuffed birds. They were worn in rakish positions held in place by lethal hatpins skewered through piled-up hairdos. To complement this costume, the hat is constructed on a buckram frame, covered in lilac silk and lace, draped with folds of iridescent lilac silk and liberally decorated with white and lavender flowers.

The golden afternoon of this Lady's garden-party world, however, would prove to be as fragile as the dainty silk and lace parasol that shielded her from the sun or the feather boa with a purely ornamental purpose. In June of 1914 a shot would ring out in Sarajevo, and the Edwardian lady would become only a lovely memory.

Plate 35

Stylish Street Toilette circa 1901

The inspiration for my Gibson Girl was a roll of cream-colored braid that, with its swirling pattern, seemed ideal for developing a costume of the Art Nouveau period, which preferred the curve over the straight. The bolero and skirt are cut from tan-colored wool, and lined in ivory silk taffeta. The bolero jacket has flared sleeves cut to accommodate the full-blouse sleeve and, in addition to the braid detail, the bolero edge and sleeves are bound in a matching tan silk.

The seven-gore skirt is an example of the graceful trumpet-like shaping of the period, further emphasized by the curving lines of the braid and taffeta binding. To further contribute to the ideal of the tall woman, the skirts were usually cut long, sweeping the floor, even for daywear. Such skirts could easily be soiled, but the wearers would most likely be of the carriage class, and thus not likely to come in contact with a sidewalk or street.

One of the dominant fashion features of the Belle Epoque was the blouse and, having arrived, it has never left. Of course the Edwardian version, unlike today's drip-dry models, was of extremely complex and fragile construction, and almost impossible to launder.

For the Stylish Street Toilette, the blouse is made up of rows of Valenciennes lace on a silk foundation, high-collared and fashionably "pouched" (to disguise the two-ness of the breast) with a cascade of gathered lace and ribbon bows over the front closure. The belt is of tan silk taffeta, dipping in front and rising at the back, a variation of the Swiss belt.

The massive hat of tan silk taffeta, abloom with clusters of red flowers, is perched and pinned securely to Madame's coiffure, though she still must be alert to a sudden gust of wind in the willows. Underneath the swirling skirt is the indispensable rustling silk taffeta petticoat and, to complete the Toilette, a ubiquitous ivory silk parasol trimmed in tan lace, more a fashionable affectation than an item of service-ability.

In a list of "things to refrain from" in *A Book of Edwardian Etiquette* (by One Of The Aristocracy) ladies were advised: "Don't wear a number of diamonds or other precious stones by day; it is never in good taste." Accordingly I have allowed my Lady a pair of discreet gold earrings and a tasteful gold chain and locket.

The bolero, either sleeveless or with sleeves, was one of the most representative of Edwardian garments. It was made of any material, from lace to rich fur; and, worn with a skirt to match, it formed an excellent costume for showing off the pouched blouse and the forward tilt of the figure which had become the "rage" through the popularity of Charles Dana Gibson, the American black-and-white artist.

The Woman in Fashion
Doris Langley Moore

Plate 36

Bridal Gown circa 1902

One thing is certain, the skirt must
fit like wax at the top, and fall in
full, graceful folds to the feet.
THE QUEEN, 1899

In 1992 I was asked by Tiffany's of Boston to loan four of my bridal figures for their window display during the bridal month. Instead of four brides, I created a bridal group consisting of the bride, her bridesmaid, her mother and her trousseau negligee, or tea gown, all circa 1902. In the Bridal Gown I tried to capture the unique style and elegant charm of Edwardian fashions. The fabric is a soft silk

peau d'ange (angel skin), lined in silk organdy. The bodice is high-necked and long-sleeved, with the required pouch and downward slant in front. To accent the full-bosomed mode, I used a bertha of finely pleated Chantilly lace, which appears from beneath a row of delicate border lace and pearl-trimmed bows.

With the admonishing quote from the Queen in mind, I carefully cut and fitted the skirt gores to assure a "wax-like" fit, and to be sure that the folds would be full and graceful. A deep flounce of the pleated lace surrounds the sweeping hemline with a heading of the border lace and silk bows. The Gibson Girl's coiffure is crowned with a wreath of wax orange blossoms and a long silk tulle veil.

It was Sir Winston Churchill who wrote in his memoirs that: "The Old World in its sunset was fair to see." It was the world of La Belle Epoque to which he referred, and this Edwardian bridal dress is a reflection of the fashions of that sunset world that Sir Winston found so fair.

Plate 37

Bridesmaid's Gown circa 1902

The article goes on to advise that the bridesmaid dresses should be "dainty and pretty, though of a less handsome and striking material than your own gown." It also advises that the bride should "try to select something that will be of use after the one great occasion." As I read it, I experienced déjà vu, for this bit of advice must have been written in stone as it still reverberates within the walls of bridal salons from coast to coast. Ninety-nine percent of ex-bridesmaids usually find their storage closets a little tighter after the "great occasion."

The 1902 Bridesmaid's Gown is in a "dainty" shade of blue created by a layer of cream-colored dotted net over blue silk *peau de soie*. The bodice has a standing collar of crystal pleated *point d'esprit*, and a sheer yoke of dotted net with a square bertha of pleated point d'esprit and appliqués of tape lace. Pleated *point d'esprit*

and blue silk *peau de soie* finish the elbow-length sleeves. A blue silk belt encircles the wasp waist, accenting the long bodice line.

The skirt is fashionably gored with bands of Valenciennes lace covering the seams and the curving line where the dotted net flounce, appliquéd with tape lace, swirls in a mass of frou-frou at the hem. Rows of pleated silk organdy and *point d'esprit*, in addition to appliqués of tape lace and blue ostrich feathers, bedeck a dashing hat of blue silk.

The only jewelry is a pair of blue crystal earrings and a gold pin in a heart design at the throat. According to the April 1898 *Harper's Bazar* a "pretty pin or ring is the best thing you can give to your bridesmaids."

Possibly this ensemble, after serving its initial purpose would, with the addition of a matching parasol, be quite charming for the Lady's next garden party. As to whether it detracts from the bride's costume, I will leave that question to the eye of the beholder.

Plate 38

The Mother of the Bride circa 1902

The gown that the mother-of-the-bride shall wear is of a great deal of importance, for she is next to the most conspicuous figure, or rather should be, at every wedding, and her gown of course will be more or less observed.

HARPER'S BAZAR, APRIL 2, 1898

I t was a society mother's duty to marry off her daughters, and to marry them off well, meaning at least into their own social world, or possibly a step higher. If that failed, there was always Europe and the satisfaction of a title (the purchase of which was not considered demeaning). A reference to "my daughter, the duchess" was such a lovely phrase to drop among the tinkle of teacups.

The wedding ceremony represented the culmination of a year or two of intense plotting and labor and for this, her moment of triumph, she deserved to be conspicuous, observed and clothed in splendor. One of the colors considered appropriate for a mother's gown was of the heliotrope family and, as luck would have it, I just happened to have in my inventory a piece of pale-lilac silk satin which seemed quite suitable. Also among my collection of lace was a beautiful piece of *point de gaze* that I felt that any mother would love to wear, and that would certainly be "conspicuous."

The dress consists of a separate bodice and skirt, but is designed in the semi-princess style (also recommended by *Harper's Bazar* as a "smart" look for mothers). In this case, this princess line is achieved by the application of the lace beginning with the standing collar edged with pleated tulle. From there the lace descends over the bust to a deep V at the center front, blending into the skirt panel. The shaped belt disappears under the lace on one side, reappearing under the large bow on the other and continuing on to the center back. The sleeves are long and appliquéd with lace, finished at the wrist with pleated silk tulle. A crossed bow, with pearl and amethyst center, is placed at one shoulder, complementing the one at the opposite waist.

The skirt is composed of seven fitted gores with the center gore of *point de gaze* lace over lilac satin, completing the effect of a neck-to-hem princess panel. This panel is outlined with cording and decorated with two large crossed bows near the hem. The skirt is lined in lilac silk organdy and finished with satin cording. There is also a *balayeuse* of pleated ivory lace.

The petticoat for this costume is of lilac taffeta with a deep pleated flounce of purple taffeta. By the turn of the century, the rustling taffeta petticoats were being produced in all sorts of colors (even naughty black), which made the fleeting glimpse even more exciting.

For accessories there is a striking hat of lilac silk, antique lace and purple ostrich feathers. The jewelry consists of drop pearl and amethyst earrings, and a necklace of two strands of pearl and amethyst beads. The fan is of lilac silk organdy and antique lace with hand-painted sticks.

Mama in this silvery-lilac gown with its opulent display of magnificent lace could proceed by stately measured steps down the aisle with an inner glow of satisfaction at having accomplished her mission. As for a few envious glances from the assembled guests—she could consider it frosting on the cake!

Plate 39

Trousseau Negligee or Tea Gown circa 1902

Those ladies of the demimonde were not supposed to exist as far as the ladies of Mrs. Pritchard's circle were concerned; however she did not discount their influence when advising her readers that pretty lingerie was a means of husband control. Therefore I clothed the fourth figure in my 1992 group for Tiffany's of Boston in the bride's Trousseau Negligee.

Negligees and tea gowns reached a peak of extreme extravagance during the Edwardian years, when luxurious and delicate fabrics were blended into exotic confections of "French frivolity" and elegance. This trousseau piece is composed of yards of fragile princess lace, backed with ivory cotton net, over a lining of pale-pink silk taffeta and silk organdy. The bodice is cut with an Empire-style waist, and a silk taffeta collar with a standing ruffle of pleated *point d'esprit*. Appliqués of lace flowers trail from the shoulders to the bow at the pink silk waistband, and on to the hem of the skirt. The full bishop-style sleeves are caught in with a silk band and bow at the wrist, ending in a ruffle of pleated *point d'esprit*. The open skirt falls from the waistband in lavish folds over a petticoat of pink silk taffeta trimmed with ruffles of cream-colored pleated lace.

As an insurance to preserve a husband's fidelity, Mrs. Pritchard's advice seems a bit shortsighted, for the same garments were available to those "less-favored women," and supplied by the same husbands. *C'est la vie!*

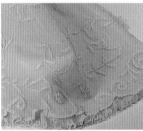

Plate 40

Lingerie Dress circa 1904

To most ears "lingerie" means lace and elaborateness. Literally it means anything that is linen, but everyday parlance applies the term to any kind of a thin frock that is not silk and which can visit the laundry.

"Mrs. Osborn's Letter"
THE DELINEATOR, JULY 1908

*T*hese words were written in 1908 by Mrs. Osborn, a fashion oracle for *The Delineator* and owner of a fashion establishment in New York. She writes with disarming simplicity of the lovely and intricate white dresses so much in vogue during the Edwardian years, which were known as Lingerie Dresses. The term came from the delicate lingerie-like construction of these summer dresses. Made of lawn, batiste, eyelet or any fine lightweight cotton, they were assembled with all kinds of intricate lace insertions, tucking and embroidery. They were evidently very popular and well made, judging from the number one finds in collections and vintage-clothing shops.

To create a Lingerie Dress for my collection I used an old turn-of-the-century petticoat that had all the decorative details required for this type of dress. The skirt is cut directly from the petticoat, including the flounce, and carefully eased into the waistband. There is only a center back seam where the insertion bands meet in a slight V. The skirt is further embellished with a trailing appliqué of lace flowers and bows, very lightly embroidered with chalk beads. There is a separate slip of white silk taffeta with a deep lace-bordered flounce, plus a petticoat made up from the flounce of another sample of my antique-petticoat inventory.

The waist is cut from the remaining section of the original petticoat with a full pouched front and a yoke of Irish lace and val-lace ruffles. The Irish lace also forms the proscribed high collar—not very comfortable on a hot muggy day but that was the price of fashion.

The belt is of blue silk, cut low in the front and quite high in the back. A narrow drape of lavender silk goes from front to back, ending in a triple-loop bow decorated with chalk and lavender glass beads. A similar treatment of blue and lavender silk is also used at the wrist of the full sleeves.

A wide-brimmed hat is covered in blue silk and decorated with white lilacs, lace and lavender ribbons. The Lady carries a white eyelet parasol with a handle of ivory in the shape of a little dog's head. A small purse of blue silk sprinkled with chalk beads provides Madame with a few coins should an occasion necessitating a charitable donation arise.

Keeping such frocks fresh and pristine was no easy task, requiring the services of an army of frustrated laundresses and ladies' maids. However, Madame would have been oblivious of such mundane matters as she appeared in un-mussed and elegant perfection in her fashionable and exclusive world.

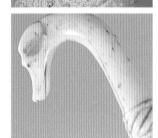

Plate 41

Tea Gown circa 1906

During the revolution a group of patriots decked out in feathers and buckskin, as sham Indians, managed to begin the pollution of Boston harbor with bales of British tea, and thus the republic was born. However, despite this rebellious act and the fact that the ultraconservative society of old New York and Boston would, for the next several generations, regard things Continental (and especially British) as decadent, the very English custom of afternoon tea survived the fracas, and become one of the important rituals of the new American aristocracy.

The tea gown appeared around the mid-1870s as a loose-fitting garment to slip into for the leisurely tea hour at home, before dressing for the evening's activities. *The Delineator* showed "pretty wrappers" suitable for the occasion, but the great dressmakers quickly transformed it into another garment of conspicuous consumption.

To create a poetical tea gown in keeping with Mrs. Pritchard's lyrical description, I hand-applied an assortment of antique laces on cream-colored dotted net, backed with mauve silk taffeta. Then I lightly gathered a plastron of lace and dotted net over the bodice into a folded band of silk, which rises from the center front waist to the shoulder-blade area at the back. A narrow guipure-type lace proceeds from the top of the shoulder along the plastron edge, slipping under the silk waist-

band and continuing down the skirt to frame the faux-petticoat front panel.

A row of the same narrow lace appears above the delicate lace flounce that extends around the sides and back of the skirt. At the center back, where the folds of the silk waistband join, there is a pretty motif of multi-colored embroidery, satin ribbons and long trailing streamers of crochet work. At this same place two lace panels are gathered into a Watteau-style back treatment that flows into the short train. The sleeves are puffed and gathered into a silk band from which falls a full gathered lace flounce.

A matching set of jewelry consists of a four-strand necklace, earrings and bracelets, all of pearl and amethyst.

A lady attired in such a Tea Gown, ensconced amid the white-and-gold décor of her quasi-Louis XVI drawing room, relaxing over her tea before undertaking the ordeal of dressing for dinner, is perhaps the ultimate expression of the leisurely and lavish existence enjoyed by Edwardian aristocracy.

Plate 42

Dinner at the Paris Ritz circa 1906

By this time it was no longer a social taboo for ladies to dine in public, and the elegant Hotel Ritz provided an opulent setting for fashionable display. The Gilded Age was never embarrassed by a display of wealth—such a display was encouraged.

For sheer extravagance, I used a layering technique of two laces: a fine black silk lace over a cream-colored lace, both of a floral pattern, one blending into the other. Another lace with a scallop-border pattern is used on the wide collar and hem of the skirt. Combined with this border lace are a series of embroidered appliqués from a box of bits and pieces in my burgeoning inventory. These appliqués consist of a soft-pink flower caught with a blue bow and framed with black-and-cream scrollwork. They were lined with a shattered pink silk, which I removed before appliquéing them to the lace. Showing beneath the scalloped lace at the hem is a ruching of dotted net over crystal pleated cream-colored lace, both attached to the ivory silk taffeta slip. To further contribute to this conspicuous consumption of expensive and fragile materials, which by their very nature will only afford a limited period of wear, the black lace is laboriously hand-applied with tiny iridescent sequins for a touch of refined glitter.

The crowning glory of this ensemble is, without doubt, the spectacular black velvet hat with its sweeping arrangement of pink and black ostrich plumes. A black-sequin trim edges the brim, and an ornament of faux diamonds decorates a black silk taffeta bow. These sumptuous millinery confections would become world famous in 1907 with the production of Franz Lehars' incomparable *The Merry Widow*, a musical homage to La Belle Epoque.

For jewelry, the Lady wears a choker of black velvet decorated with steel-cut disks and beads and matching earrings. A black velvet belt, bound in silk taffeta, aids in minimizing the waistline and, hidden from view, is a lace-trimmed petticoat of cream silk taffeta "veiled" with black silk organdy and black pleated *point d'esprit*. The shoes are of black silk satin.

At the entrance to the dining room Madame pauses to carefully adjust her black velvet stole, and to allow her fellow diners sufficient time to observe and admire, discreetly, her ravishing toilette. How she will manage to consume one of the hotel's copious dinners is unknown, but her thoughtfully arranged grand entrance should more than adequately compensate for any digestive inconvenience.

Plate 43

Robe de Style circa 1906

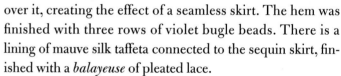

The Princess could write with authority, for not only was she part of these past glories, but her royal and imperial intimacies guaranteed her entrée to every palace in Europe and invitations to as many parties as she chose to grace. As far as "lavish" and "pageants," the extravagant Edwardian society was one endless and lavish pageant that provided a splendid setting in which ladies could appear, shimmering from head to toe, in gowns such as this.

A violet sequin dress worn by Queen Alexandra, the consort of Edward VII, which I saw at an exhibit of Belle Epoque costume at The Metropolitan Museum, was the inspiration for this Robe de Style. The sequin embroidery was done by an expert beader who worked with me at Priscilla of Boston. The technique is called "tambour beading." Each piece of the garment is outlined on a square of lilac silk organdy. These pieces are then carefully pinned to a wooden frame, with the marking face up. With her left hand, the beader feeds up the sequins or beads (which are on a thread) from underneath the frame to the fabric, while with the right hand a tambour hook (similar to a crochet hook) is pushed through the fabric, catching the thread and pulling the sequin, or bead, into place. The embroidery for this dress required approximately two hundred hours to complete.

Each beaded section was then cut out and sewn together. The skirt is composed of eleven shaped gores, and the sequin beading is separated by radiating lines of violet beads. As each seam was sewn together, a row of violet beads was hand-sewn

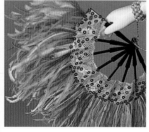

over it, creating the effect of a seamless skirt. The hem was finished with three rows of violet bugle beads. There is a lining of mauve silk taffeta connected to the sequin skirt, finished with a *balayeuse* of pleated lace.

The sequin bodice is cut low, with shoulder straps of violet silk satin and short sequin sleeves, which are finished with beaded fringe. Bows of the violet satin are placed at the point where the shoulder straps and sleeves join. On the front right bow is an amethyst-and-diamond star-shaped brooch. A second brooch secures a headpiece of violet ostrich feathers. The jewelry is of pearls, amethyst and diamonds; the shaped belt is of violet silk satin, and the fan of sequined lace and ostrich feathers.

The memoirs of the Princess paint a charming and fascinating picture of Edwardian high-life and the world of the rich, but her dreams of an Anglo-German rapprochement turned out to be the century's first nightmare, and the demise of her privileged world.

Plate 44

Ball Gown circa 1906

Making an entrance at some grand ball, arrayed in the shimmering splendor of sequins and crowned in diamonds, an Edwardian lady's thoughts would have been far removed from the appalling conditions that contributed to her dazzling appearance. Sweating was a working condition in which hundreds of poor women beaded and embroidered by hand in old, dark and dirty buildings for long hours and extremely low pay. Work was spasmodic and, being unskilled at anything else, they led an existence of constant economic distress, at the mercy of their employer. The period was not Belle for all.

This Ball Gown is another example of tambour beading, executed on panels of black silk net in a vermicelli pattern of black, silver and iris sequins. It was done for me by the same lady who executed the Robe de Style (Plate 43). The sequins graduate from black, at the bottom of the dress, to iris and silver at the top. The black net is backed with a layer of pale-lilac silk organdy, which is laid over a slip of white silk taffeta.

The hem of the skirt is composed of three flounces—a pleated black *point d'esprit*, a gathered silk organdy and a pleated silk taffeta. There is also a *balayuese* of pleated lace. Where the flounce and skirt join, there is a row of black lace roses.

The bodice is cut off the shoulder with shoulder straps of black velvet, and elbow-length puffed sleeves of organdy and sequined net with appliqués of black-lace scrollwork and roses. The same appliqué-work forms a loose plastron over the bosom.

There is a deep pointed belt of black velvet, bound in silk, with a decorative trim of black silk flowers and velvet streamers attached at the right side. The shoes are also done in black velvet.

For additional glitter there are earrings, a bracelet and a black velvet "dog collar," dripping with faux diamonds. The marquisite tiara was originally part of a tortoise-shell comb. I had it removed from the comb and gently curved to fit the mannequin's head, a touch-and-go operation, as the stones could have easily popped out, but it was one of those "lucky" days! The final accessory is a lush black-feather stole, weighted at the ends with clusters of jet balls and silk satin ribbons.

If at all aware of the dark side of the Belle Epoque, or troubled by that state of affairs, the lady of fashion could do her duty by patronizing the deserving poor with well-meaning acts of charity. They, in turn, were suppose to work hard to improve their lot, and not make a tiresome fuss that would upset the natural order of things.

Plate 45

The Ascot Toilette circa 1907

There she stands in familiar silhouette—rigidly corseted, swathed in rustling silks, The wide hat on puffed-out hair, gloved hand holding a parasol. In hundreds of photographs and paintings she stares coolly at us, her thoughts concealed behind that splendidly maintained façade.

The Edwardian Lady
KATE CAFFREY

And where better to show off that "splendid facade" than at the Ascot Races, the sport of kings? The gentlemen came for the sport, and the ladies for the promenade of fashion. This costume is actually my interpretation of the Ascot Race scene from that musical evocation of the Belle Epoque, *My Fair Lady*; although the fashions shown in the film were of a later date (1912–14), for me the black-and-cream color scheme is enough to capture the moment.

The fabric choice for the costume is a cream silk faille, black grosgrain ribbon and organdy cutwork. The skirt is made up of eleven princess gores, which begin just under the bust line, and fall from there into a flaring skirt. By 1907 the dressmakers were once more suggesting a return of the high-waisted Empire line, one of those historical revivals that fashion attempts every so often, and which would be hardly recognizable to a lady of that particular epoch. However, the high join-line of this skirt and bodice would be enough to convince an Edwardian wearer that she was recapturing a style associated with the Empress Josephine and the First Empire.

At the foot of the skirt are two bias folds of faille alternating with two bands of black grosgrain ribbon. Over these is applied a garland of ivory lace accented with jet

beading. The petticoat is of ivory silk taffeta with a deep flounce of several yards of pleated *point d'esprit*.

An over-drape, creating a jumper-like appearance to the costume, rises from the high waistline over the shoulder to the center back. It is of faille, bound in black grosgrain ribbon, and appliquéd with an elaborate jet passementerie. Beneath it is a long-sleeved bodice of organdy cutwork, with a jet-trimmed standing collar. Both the collar and sleeves are finished with frills of pleated *point d'esprit*.

To complete this Ascot Toilette there is a black feather boa with silk tassel ends, cream faille shoes with black satin bows and a cream-and-black-trimmed silk parasol. The wide-brimmed hat of cream faille and organdy cutwork is trimmed with black satin ribbon, black velvet flowers and an assortment of black feathers. If the Lady's stare is cool and her thoughts appear concealed it is probably because she is totally absorbed in the management of all this splendor.

Plate 46

The Tailor-made Suit circa 1908

*I*n the early years of the century, the elaborately gowned Edwardian lady discovered she had a rival—the "New Woman" in her tailor-made costume. The uncluttered suit was thought ideal for the sportswoman, the bicyclist and those adventurous young women who were to become known as "Career Girls." However, this wine-colored wool costume is more for the society lady who, not unadventurous herself, wore her tailor-made for shopping excursions, luncheons at the Ritz and even quiet weddings.

The elegantly cut jacket is smartly double-breasted, with steel-cut buttons, and sleeve cuffs and shawl collar of silk velvet. The lining of the jacket is mauve silk taffeta, and the curving line of the jacket skirt, which dips deeply at the back, is edged in wool cording.

The wool skirt is cut in nine gores, flaring at the hem in a series of velvet-lined box pleats. The high waistband is cut in one with the skirt gores and finished with cording. Beneath the wool and velvet skirt lurks a very feminine petticoat of ivory silk

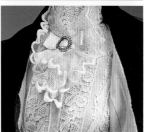

taffeta and lace, and boots of velvet and grosgrain.

The blouse is of mauve silk with a front inset panel and standing collar of antique lace. The rather masculine appearance of the costume is softened by a very frilly jabot and circle brooch of marquisite.

In order to assure the wearer of not being mistaken for one of those New Women or, worse still, a Career Girl, the accessories accompanying this particular tailor-made suit are in typically Edwardian high style. A large, luxurious fur muff of seal skin, trimmed with passementerie, protects delicate work-free fingers from the fall frost, and a magnificent black satin hat, adorned with a sweeping arrangement of iridescent coq feathers, is worn at a daringly rakish angle, secured in place with long lethal hat pins.

Despite its simplicity of cut, the cachet of a suit of this quality, in a society so absorbed with social distinctions, was that everyone who mattered would be acutely aware of how expensive it was.

Plate 47

Garden Party Toilette circa 1909

Perhaps if one kept busy and cheerful and enjoyed everything, the danger—if danger there was— would go away.

The Edwardian Lady
KATE CAFFREY

*A*lthough La Belle Epoque had another five years to go, at the close of the new century's first decade change was in the air. Revolutionary movements rumbled about in Russia and the Balkans, and the Kaiser was rattling his saber in a rather belligerent manner. But the Edwardian society drifted on in its languorous way, indifferent to any change save that of fashion.

By 1909 the direction of fashion was toward a slimmer line. Skirts had less fullness, falling in soft folds to the ground; sleeves were long and fitted, and bodices high-waisted, quasi-Empire. However, fabrics were as luxurious and elegant as ever.

Lace, at this period, was one of the most fashionable choices for race and garden-party dresses, which determined my selection of a beautiful ivory corded lace for this Garden Party Toilette, combined with pale-blue silk.

The richness of the lace demanded very little embellishment, but this was the Edwardian period and I don't believe the term "basic" was part of their vocabulary. A wide elaborate frill of narrow guipure lace and gathered val circles the bodice, dipping low in front, emphasizing the mono-bosom mode that was still in vogue.

The lace skirt is cut in five sections, each one backed with a layer of cotton net. The hem is finished with the narrow guipure and gathered val. The slip is cut in similar sections of pale-blue silk *peau de soie*, with the hem finished in gathered val lace. There is a slim ivory silk taffeta petticoat with an elaborate flounce of val lace and satin ribbons. The high waist is accented with a sash and double bows of pale-blue silk satin. There are two satin streamers at the center back, the ends of which are decorated with bows and hand-crocheted ornaments. Shoes are ivory silk decorated with blue satin ribbon.

As the silhouette became slimmer, hats became larger. This model of silk and lace with a wide turned-down brim was one of the prevailing styles of 1909. The excessive use of plumage was wreaking havoc among the bird population; the Audubon Society was up in arms, and even attacking hats!

For jewelry there are two long ropes of pearl and crystal, and a pair of delicate drop earrings. A parasol of ivory silk taffeta and lace with a lovely carved handle completes the Toilette, and allows Madame to affect a pose of regal serenity.

This gown could be regarded as one of those transitional styles that appears as the fashion of one period moves into the next. Despite the elegance of the lace, the line of the gown is relatively simple, compared with the frilly and detailed exuberance of the preceding years. The only hint of the coming mode is the size of the hat, which will become even larger and more elaborate during the early years of the next decade.

Plate 48

Robe d'Après-Midi circa 1910

I am often asked about the motivation for a costume and, in most cases, it is a certain fabric or lace that suggests a particular period, or the need to add a specific style missing from the collection. However, in the case of the Robe d'Après-Midi it happens to be the little leather-bound engagement book, embossed in gold with the year "1910," that the Lady is holding. I thought it needed a dress to go with it!

By 1910 the fashionable silhouette had become quite sheath-like, and the notorious hobble skirt was sending shock waves through the world of high fashion. In its extreme form it was only worn by the ultra avant-garde; the more conservative versions were equipped with hidden godets, or pleats, to allow for some walking latitude, or the graceful ascending of a staircase.

For Madame's afternoon engagement, I have used a black silk net embroidered with extremely fine, silvery-gold metallic thread, accented with a bead-like white thread design, in a swirling pattern. This is a combination of a four-and-three-quarter-inch border and a seven-inch galloon embroidery.

The bodice and long fitted sleeves are cut in one, in ivory silk organdy, to which the embroidered sections are applied. The high collar is of black silk satin, bound in off-white silk taffeta, with a frill of black silk net. The edges of the sleeves are finished with a band of off-white silk and a frill of black net.

The bodice is softly gathered into the raised waistline and attached to the skirt. A wide belt of black silk satin closes at one side with a bow on which is centered a diamante circle pin.

The sheath skirt, backed with silk organdy, is made up of four straight panels of the border embroidery, with inset triangular side panels framed in folds of off-white silk taffeta. These triangular panels allow for the aforementioned walking latitude. There is a slip of silk taffeta with a pleated hem and a narrow petticoat of dotted net. Shoes are of black leather (from an old pair of gloves) with silver buckles.

The circumference of the hat is more than that of the skirt, an accepted proportion of the day that represents one of fashion's illogical mysteries. This splendid millinery creation is off-white silk, accented with large loops of black satin ribbon, a circle of diamante glitter and an explosion of black and cream ostrich feathers.

The ladies attending the famous Black Ascot appeared in mourning dress in honor of the late King, but I think that this elegantly subdued costume would have pleased His Majesty, who had a keen eye for a beautiful woman dressed in high fashion.

Plate 49

Toilette de Promenade circa 1910

*T*he elegant Parisian ladies of La Belle Epoque appeared in the Bois de Boulogne every day between eleven and noon, or later in the day at the Journée des Drags (races), in their most spectacular ensembles. By 1910 Poiret's new straight tubular line was "à la mode" and the former curves were "démodé!" Although not very conducive to a brisk stroll, the new style was quite perfect for a leisurely promenade, or for observing the horses at Auteuil—both events of great social importance.

Some time ago I came across this interesting fabric: a delicate fern-patterned black Chantilly lace appliquéd with an off-white-and-black floral printed chiffon. It appeared to have been part of a skirt, with several long darts already taken apart. The mix of textures fascinated me and, as in the case of the fabric of the preceding Robe d'Après Midi, seemed compatible with the 1910 period.

The construction of the dress is also similar to the Robe d'Après-Midi; the bodice and sleeves are cut in one and joined to the straight skirt. The problem, however, was how to best take advantage of the fabric design, at the same time watching the grain, and avoiding the cut-out darts. This required a process I call "romancing the fabric," which means I spend a day or more contemplating the fabric design and moving the pattern pieces around for different effects, praying that the final choice is the best one. In this type of situation, once the fabric has been cut, there is no second chance.

In this case, the final choice did work, although I had to cut out and appliqué a few chiffon flowers to complete the wandering floral design. The lace and chiffon is backed with ivory silk organdy, and there is a slip of ivory silk satin. The narrow petticoat is of black *point d'esprit* with a flounce of pleated lace and trimmed in pink grosgrain ribbon. The shoes are black silk satin.

The chiffon hem is finished with a band of black satin ribbon, which is also used to finish the sleeves. There is a belt of the same ribbon, trimmed at the front and back with rosettes of the floral chiffon. Concealing the skirt opening are two long ribbon streamers finished with jet beading.

The "toplofty" creation precariously placed on her head is a huge mushroom-shaped confection of ivory silk overlaid with black lace and adorned with four large black silk bows. The contrast of the grandiose hat with the slim tubular dress seems incongruous, as does the need for a parasol, but it is all part of that opulent spectacle that was La Belle Epoque. Or, in the words of the photographer Latique: "How could I not have been enthralled by those great ladies in their sumptuous clothes. Their extravagant hats particularly fascinated me." (How indeed!)

Such toplofty creations imposed a statuesque dignity on bearers. How could even the flightiest girl forget that she had balanced on her head this precarious accessory which even the slightest sudden impulsive movement might disconcertingly dislodge?

J.H. Latique
EDITA S.A. & J.H. LATIQUE

Plate 50

Casino Toilette circa 1911

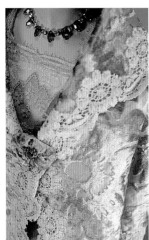

S ociety had been dazzled by the unexpected spectacle of the Ballet Russe, introduced to Paris and London between 1910 and 1911. The brilliant oriental colors overshadowed the pale pastels of the Edwardian palette, and the exotic East became fashion's inspiration, led by the avant-garde designer Paul Poiret.

I obtained the fabric for this costume from a lady whose mother sewed and had a passion for beautiful materials and, fortunately, a large-enough house to accommodate her collecting mania. The dress fabric is a lovely blue-and-cream silk tulle, woven with an interesting pattern of blue-and-silver motifs of oriental influence. The bodice and skirt are backed with a pale-blue silk organdy, over a slip of ivory silk taffeta. The pleated sash is of moiré silk with two long floating panels in the back.

Accompanying the dress is a luxurious evening coat cut in the new kimono fashion, in a soft silvery-gold lamé and blue velvet. (This gorgeous material was also from the same lady's collection, and I certainly appreciate her good taste!) The shawl collar, sleeves and coat are bordered with antique ivory lace and lined with ivory silk taffeta. The coat is closed in front with a self-fabric button, centered with dull-gold and blue beads. The shoes are ivory satin with blue bows.

In my flea-market/antique-shop excursions, I always poke through any displays of old costume jewelry, looking for bits and pieces that can be adapted into jewels for Les Dames. In one such instance I found this necklace set with blue stones in just the right scale. With a few snips of my jeweler's pliers, I created a "sapphire" necklace and earrings worthy of Monte Carlo (providing Madame does not try to sell them to pay off her gambling losses!).

To complete the oriental mood of the Toilette is a toque of draped silk and tulle—a turban fit for a sultana of the western world. For a restless and leisured society, dressing up for every occasion to be seen was one of its most constant pleasures, and the Casino at Monte Carlo must have provided a spectacular backdrop.

Plate 51

The Voyage circa 1912

S he stands comfortably assured, surrounded by bits and pieces of her elegantly labeled luggage and her properly groomed dog, about to board the most luxurious ship in the world. For my Lady's bon-voyage costume I thought a smart two-piece ensemble in the form of a dress and matching jacket would be a suitable selection. The fabrics are a deep-ivory-and-black-striped silk, black silk taffeta, black lace and trim of black braid.

The black lace bodice is lined with ivory silk, and is lightly eased into the high-waisted skirt under a band of black silk satin. The sleeves are finished with a similar band of satin and lace edging. The same lace edging forms a standing collar at the neckline.

The striped skirt is cut "à la hobble," very close to the figure, terminating in a curving line at knee level, dipping toward the back. What appears to be an underskirt of black silk taffeta continues on to the hem with the join line concealed by a row of braid and self-fabric fringe. At both sides of the taffeta section are pleated inserts, otherwise Madame's navigation of the gangplank could be a rather difficult and undignified experience. A delicate lace petticoat serves propriety, and the shoes are of cream-colored leather.

The kimono-style jacket is of Japanese origin and, although very chic, probably as confining by design as the hobble skirt. For a member of the leisured class, however, effect would supercede comfort. The edge of the jacket is finished with black braid, and the ends of the wide collar are accented with passementerie and clusters of silk balls. A bow of the black silk taffeta covers the jacket closing.

Smaller hats were now beginning to displace the huge plumed and floral structures that had been in favor during the first decade. This draped silk taffeta with one soaring feather seems a suitable choice for a rather avant-garde ensemble. Hats may have been becoming smaller but, for some inexplicable reason, large decorative muffs of a completely unserviceable nature became a fashionable accessory.

In a very short time the costume, luggage and fluffy pet will sink to the bottom of the North Atlantic. The Lady will find herself huddled in a cold and classless lifeboat wondering whatever happened to the exclusive and privileged world she had always known—and would it ever be the same again?

I only realized the gravity of the situation when I saw a third class passenger on the first class deck. (From a survivor aboard the Titanic)

The Belle Epoque: Trends and Developments
PAOLO MONELLI

Plate 52

Grande Robe de Soie circa 1913

The source of the fabric for the Casino Toilette was also the source for this pale-turquoise and coral Art-Deco-style beading. As I looked through her textile collection, I came across a narrow roll (two-and-a-half inches by six yards) of beading stuffed in the bottom of a box. It obviously had never been used but was still quite fragile, the beads having been applied to a very fine silk tulle. Beading that was done at that period was often executed on very delicate materials, which accounts for their poor survival rate. Although the asking price was high I knew that it was meant for one of my Ladies—and for them, only the best! At the time I did not have anything in mind for its use, but once I found myself involved with the 1910–1914 period I knew why I had unflinchingly made the investment.

To stabilize and distribute the weight of the embroidery, I first cut all the pattern pieces in ivory cotton net. I then cut out strips of the embroidery and hand-applied each section to the net, tacking them down carefully.

I cut through the beading with trepidation, wondering how many beads were going to fall off, or if the whole thing would begin to unravel. Fortunately, only a few beads were lost and beneath those, I was fascinated to discover the original pencil guide lines used by the beaders. (This discovery gave me a rather eerie feeling that I was communicating with the person who did this beautiful work so long ago, and I wanted to be sure my dress would be equal to her craftsmanship.)

The sheath-like design was perfect for the placement of the beaded panels, with a single piece across the lower front. This band disappears under the two longer back panels, which extend into a demi-train of fashionable, but impractical, proportion. A "rain" of shimmering crystal fringe (three inches in length) hangs from the horizontal band. I found this fringe (also used on the 1885 Wedding Gown, Plate 19) stuffed in a plastic bag, soaked in condensation, on the ground at a local flea market. Moral of the story—always keep your mind and eyes open and, in this case, your nose to the ground! Beneath the fringe is a piece of very fine ivory lace to add texture and to veil the silk satin slip.

The bodice is attached to the skirt under the folded satin waistband, which closes at the center back under a satin *choux* (rosette). The beading is placed in

a V-like position with an insert section across the front. The fine lace fills in the bodice sides and extends the beaded sleeves to just above the elbow, and is hidden by another rain of crystal fringe.

A long necklace of pearl and crystal extends to the waist, and crystal drop earrings appear from beneath a demi-turban of the beaded embroidery, surmounted by a lavish spray of feathers. To add more drama to an already dramatic ensemble, I added a huge fan of white feathers.

Only a lady of unlimited means (or a demimondaine with a rich protector) could afford an original designed couture dress of this quality, which would cost more than a seamstress earned in a year. Despite the cost, its fragile nature and striking appearance would limit its wearablility in the small and exclusive circle of society to which its wearer belonged. This, however, was not for a grande dame of La Belle Epoque to ponder, and as far as the inconvenience of the restricting design—well, there would always be a gentleman available for assistance.

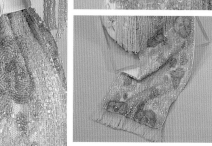

Plate 53

Afternoon Frock circa 1914

O
ne could also add that this practical design was a possible solution for those who felt that the figure-revealing new skirts were too revealing! (Avoirdupois can be a trying problem for a lady of fashion). Another revolutionary design change was the "low neckline" which finally replaced the standard daytime high collar of the past several decades. Modestly round, square or V-shaped, it nevertheless appalled the clergy, and doctors predicted a pneumonia epidemic, but the ladies, as usual, turned a deaf ear.

For this dressy Afternoon Frock for a fashionable lady of leisure, I chose a rich coffee-colored lace over ivory silk satin, with an accent color of shell-pink satin.

The dress is designed in two parts; a lace overdress and a satin under-dress. The satin portion is in the form of a fitted strapless bodice joined to one of the new draped skirts, as shown in the pattern drafting instructions entitled *Thornton's International System* (1913). Although the Thornton version does not show a walking slit, I inserted a pleated section low at the center back, despite which small, mincing steps would still be required.

The kimono-style bodice of the lace overdress is all cut in one with a V-inset of lace at both front and back, forming one of those "scandalous" low necklines, which is framed with wide lace revers. Also cut in one is the lace tunic, straight across the front into a deep point at the center back. The join line of the bodice and tunic is concealed by a shell-pink satin sash with a satin rosette placed at the center front where the revers meet. At the back is a large satin butterfly bow and two sash ends, weighted down by large tassels, whose undulating movements could be another source of clerical disapproval.

Attached to the sash is a charming silver purse, another antique-shop find. (There would be barely enough room for the wearer in this style of skirt, let alone a pocket).

The simplicity of this frock is misleading, for its complicated back closure of hooks and snaps could only be accomplished by the assistance of a lady's maid. If one could afford these dresses, however, one could certainly retain the services of a maid—or two.

For accessories, a simple pearl choker and pearl drop earrings adhere to the caution that too much display of jewels during the day would be considered a fashion faux pas. The parasol is ivory silk covered with coffee-colored lace. The shoes are ivory silk satin with fringed and gold-beaded bows.

The style of the hat for this costume was referred to by *The Criterion of Fashion* in December 1913 as a "pork pie" or "pot" turban, a rather undignified descriptive term, considering the elegance of the ensemble. An inverted flowerpot does come to mind, but only briefly, if one concentrates on the velvet and satin flowers, and the artistic draping and bow of shell-pink satin ribbon. A "pot" shape, maybe, but so chic!

In 1914 tight skirts, exposed necklines, tunics and tassels were causing a tempest in the teapot of fashion. But in August of that same year, a much more serious tempest would engulf the world and the extravagances of La Belle Epoque and The Gilded Age would be no more.

The tunic design is one of the most graceful of its kind, and at the same time is simple and practical in the extreme.
McCALL's, March 1910

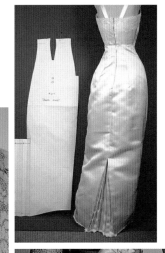

Chapter 7

Ladies in Retirement

The Ladies in Retirement are ten costumes I created twenty-five years ago, when I first became involved with this project. Since then, the collection has expanded to sixty-three pieces, a situation that has developed into a storage crisis.

My Ladies, when not enjoying the excitement of an exhibit before their adoring public, are relegated to two rows of shelving that occupy three walls of my workroom. (See page 138.) There they stand, side by side, shielded from light by black curtains, facing the wall and waiting quietly for another moment in their sun of adulation.

At this point they have absorbed all the available space, without crushing their finery, and, so, to resolve this problem I decided to institute a policy of retirement for those costumes of a certain age and replace them with something new. (Rather like life.) This allows me to move on with my "creative addiction," and the Ladies are overjoyed at the prospect of a new dress. (Also like life!)

Another consideration in deciding upon retirement for some of the costumes is my concern for the preservation of the collection. Textiles are particularly subject to damage caused by light, dust and age, and, although the ultimate purpose of the collection is to be seen and enjoyed, it is never too soon to start protecting it. The retirees are carefully stored in acid-free containers, with all the accessories, so that at some future date, when, hopefully the collection finds a permanent home, they can once again resume their fashionable mission.

OPPOSITE PAGE: *Evening Dress circa 1855.* **RIGHT:** *Spring Visiting Costume circa 1895.*

CLOCKWISE FROM ABOVE FAR LEFT: *Promenade Costume circa 1895; At Home Dress circa 1865; Wedding Gown circa 1895; Walking Costume circa 1865; Masked Ball circa 1900; Day Dress circa 1855; Garden Party Dress circa 1900; Walking Suit circa 1900.*

Chapter 8

Have Women, Will Travel

The Ladies' first museum appearance was in 1982 at the Wenham Museum in Wenham, Massachusetts, which is well known for its doll collection. At that time there were only sixteen Petites Dames, but at their thirty-sixth exhibit in 2002 at the Fairfield Historical Society in Fairfield, Connecticut, there were fifty-four Dames on display.

To move the present collection with all their staging accessories has become a formidable undertaking. Each figure travels upright in a heavy cardboard container that is designed to be collapsible for storage. Most of the cases are 14" x 14" x 32" high, with larger ones for the hoop-skirt costumes of the 1850s and 1860s.

The figures stand fully clothed on two-inch foam rubber, cut to the exact size of the container. A second piece of foam of the same dimension, but cut in half, locks around the neck securing the figure in place.

In addition to the fifty-three cases containing the mannequins, there are two large trunks containing various accessories (hats, fans, parasols, etc.). Depending on the exhibit space, there could be several other large containers to transport an assortment of props ranging from scale model furniture to a ballroom chandelier, and even a marble angel tombstone for the widow.

It requires three or four days to pack this production and to have it ready to be picked up by a Boston company that specializes in moving fine-art material. The Ladies have safely made their way about the United States over the years, and have always arrived at their destination with nary a mishap, ready to step on stage.

When I produced my first Lady in 1978, I never realized that I was establishing a traveling exhibit, much less a full-time occupation for my retirement years, when traditionally I am supposed to be sitting in a porch rocking chair staring at the sunset. Instead—Have Women, Will Travel!

In preparation for an exhibition such as the one at the Fairfield Historical Society in Fairfield, Connecticut, held in 2002 and featured on these pages, much advance work is required. **FROM ABOVE LEFT:** *A packing case is unfolded, placed upside-down and the bottom is set in place. The case is then turned upright and a two-inch-square foam pad is put in the bottom. A Lady, shielded by a plastic bag (primarily to protect her hair) is gently inserted. Two pieces of the foam rubber lock around the neck, which is wrapped with tissue paper. A labeled cover is placed on the case. The case is secured together by two heavy rubber bands and is now ready for shipment. After this process has been repeated about fifty times, the Petites Dames and their accoutrements await a most unglamorous truck ride.*

Research, Reference and Reading for the Costume-Addicted

For years I have been collecting books, museum catalogs, period publications and all kinds of bits and pieces relating to my obsession with period fashion, which have provided me with knowledge, inspiration and, I hope, the ability to create a look of authenticity in the work I so enjoy.

For those who would like to venture into the fascinating realm of period costume, and perhaps themselves embark on *An Adventure in Design*, I would like to share with you the titles of some of my research collection.

Each book listed has something to offer—some more than others. Also some are out of print but could be hiding on that newfangled thing called the Internet.

FAVORITES

The Opulent Era: Fashions by Worth, Doucet and Pingat by Elizabeth Ann Coleman (Thames and Hudson, 1989)

A wonderful journey through the high fashions of the Gilded Age. Not in print but well worth an Internet search. (If you know someone who has a copy—hire a hit man!)

Fashion, A History from the 18th to the 20th Century by the Kyoto Costume Institute (Taschen, 2002)

This is new and available and filled with color photographs. Very inspirational.

Patterns of Fashion Volumes I & II by Janet Arnold (Drama Book Specialists, 1977)

A must for anyone who wants to start creating.

The following titles, many of them reprints of old catalogs, are published by Dover Publications, 31 East 2nd Street, Mineola, NY 11501.

American Dress Pattern Catalog by Nancy Villa Bryk

American Victorian Costumes by Priscilla Harris Dalrymple

Bloomingdales Illustrated 1886 Catalog

English Woman's Clothing in the 19th Century by C. Willet Cunnington (originally published by Faber & Faber, London, 1937)

Fashions And Costumes From Godey's Ladies' Book by Stella Blum

Jordan Marsh Illustrated Catalog 1891

Montgomery & Ward Catalog 1895

Paris Fashions of the 1890's

Victorian and Edwardian Fashion: A Photographic Survey by Alison Gernsheim (originally published by Faber & Faber, London, 1963, under the title: *Fashion and Reality (1840–1914)*)

Victorian Fashions and Costumes from Harper's Bazar 1867–1898 by Stella Blum

Women's Fashions of the Early 1900's: New York Fashions 1909; National Cloak and Suit Company

MUSEUM EXHIBITION CATALOGS

Revolution in Fashion 1715–1815 Kyoto Costume Institute (1989)

Simply Stunning by Charles Otto Thieme, exhibition catalog for the Cincinnati Art Museum (1988)

Grace and Favor by Charles Otto Thieme, exhibition catalog for the Cincinnati Art Museum (1993)

The Underwear Story Fashion Intitute of New York and the Kyoto Museum (1982)

Evolution of Fashion 1835–1895 Kyoto Costume Museum (1980)

The Book of Costume by Millia Davenport
(Crown Publishers, 1948, 8th printing, 1968)

Bridal Fashions of the Victorian Era compiled
by Donna H. Felger (Hobby House Press, 1986)

Corsets and Crinolines by Nora Waugh (Rout-
ledge/Theater Art Books, 1954, 1970, 1993)

The Cut of Women's Clothes 1600–1930
by Nora Waugh (Faber & Faber, 1968)

*Dressing Dolls in 19th Century Fashions,
Vol. II* by Albina Bailey (Wallace-Homestead
Book Co., 1980)

Edwardian Hats—The Art of Millinery
by Madame Anna Ben-Yusof (R. L. Shep,
1933, 1992)

The Evolution of Fashion
by Margot Hamilton Hill and Peter A. Buckell
(Drama Book Specialists, 1967)

Garment Patterns for the Edwardian Lady
by Mrs. F. E. Thompson (Lacis, 1991)

Queen to Empress: 1837–1877
by Caroline Goldthrope (Metropolitan
Museum, 1988)

Victorian Fashions Volume I 1880–1890
by Hazel Ulseth & Helen Shannon (Hobby
House Press, 1988)

Victorian Fashions Volume II 1890–1900
by Hazel Ulseth & Helen Shannon (Hobby
House Press, 1989

To Marry an English Lord by Carol Mcd. Wal-
lace & Gail McColl (Workman Publishing, New
York 1989) A wonderful and hilarious view of
The Gilded Age.

*Franz Xavier Winterhalter and the Courts of
Europe 1830-1870* by Richard Ormond &
Carol Blackett-Ord (Harry N. Abrams, Inc., 1992)

The Light of the Home by Harvey Green
(Pantheon, 1983)

The Woman in Fashion by Doris Langley Moore
(Batsford Ltd., London, 1949—out of print but
well worth the search)

*Plate 16: Visiting
Costume circa 1885*

References for Quotes that Accompany the Plates

The Age of Worth by Edith Saunders (Indiana University, 1955)   Plates 1, 7

La Vie Parisienne by Joanna Richardson (Viking Press, 1971)   Plates 2, 5

Manners, Culture, and Dress of the Best American Society by Richard A. Wells, A.M. (King Richardson & Co, 1893)
    Plates 3, 11, 18

In the Courts of Memory by Lillie de Hegermann-Lindecrone (Garden City Publishing Company, 1911, 1912)   Plate 4

Queen of the Golden Age by Cornelius Vanderbilt Jr. (McGraw-Hill, 1956)   Plate 6

Victorian & Edwardian Fashion: A Photographic Survey   Plates 8, 21, 50

English Women's Clothing in the 19th Century   Plates 9, 14, 15, 24

Simply Stunning   Plate 10

To Marry an English Lord   Plates 12, 17, 32

Dress–Art At Home Series 1878 by Margaret Oliphant (1878)   Plate 13

Not All Vanity by Baroness De Stoeckl (Charles Scribner & Sons, 1952)   Plates 16, 22

The Woman in Fashion   Plates 19, 35, 46

Mourning Dress by Lou Taylor (George Allen & Unwin Publishers Ltd., 1983)   Plate 20

The Edwardian Lady by Kate Caffrey (Gordon & Cremonesi, 1979)   Plates 23, 34, 45, 47, 48

The Delineator: May 1893 (The Butterick Publishing Company)   Plate 25

The Light of the Home—An Intimate View of the Lives of Women in Victorian American   Plate 26

Fashions in London by Barbara Worsley-Gough (Allan Wingate, London, 1952)   Plate 27

Etiquette for Women: A Book of Modern Modes and Manners by One of the Aristocracy (C. Arthur Pearson, 1902;
    facsimile reprinted by Allen & Unwin, Inc., 1983)   Plates 28, 37

The Age of Innocence by Edith Wharton (D. Appleton & Co, 1920)   Plate 29

Harper's Bazar: 1896 (Harper and Brothers Publishers)   Plate 30

Victorian Fashions & Costumes from Harper's Bazar 1867–1898   Plate 31

The Delineator: 1900 (Fashions for September 1900)   Plate 33

The Queen: 1899   Plate 36

Harper's Bazar: April 2, 1898   Plate 38

The Cult of Chiffon by Mrs. Eric Pritchard (Grant Richards, 1902)   Plates 39, 41

The Delineator: July 1908 (Mrs. Osborn's Letter)   Plate 40

History of Fashion by Elizabeth Ewing (Batsford Ltd., London, 1974)   Plate 42

Can-Can & Flappers by Phillippe Julian (published in *La Belle Epoque: Fifteen Euphoric Years of European Fashion*,
    William Morrow & Co., 1978)   Plate 43

The Beaded Dress by John Edwards (published in *La Belle Epoque Costume: 1890–1914* for the Costume Society of
    England, Victoria & Albert Museum, 1968)   Plate 44

J.H. Latique by Edita S.A. & J.H. Latique (Ami Guichard Publisher, 1966)   Plate 49

The Belle Epoque: Trends & Developments by Paolo Monelli (published in *La Belle Epoque: Fifteen Euphoric Years of
    European Fashion*)   Plate 51

A Fashion for Extravagance by Sara Bowman (E. P. Dutton, 1985)   Plate 52

McCall's: 1910   Plate 53